IN AND OUT OF
PADDINGTON

IN AND OUT OF
PADDINGTON

THE STORY OF A GREAT RAILWAY STATION

MICHAEL H. C. BAKER

For my good friend John Villers,
whose friendship and expertise has been invaluable

Fonthill Media Language Policy

Fonthill Media publishes in the international English language market. One language edition is published worldwide. As there are minor differences in spelling and presentation, especially with regard to American English and British English, a policy is necessary to define which form of English to use. The Fonthill Policy is to use the form of English native to the author. Michael H. C. Baker was born and educated in the United Kingdom; therefore, British English has been adopted in this publication.

Fonthill Media Limited
Fonthill Media LLC
www.fonthillmedia.com
office@fonthillmedia.com

First published in the United Kingdom and the United States of America 2018

British Library Cataloguing in Publication Data:
A catalogue record for this book is available from the British Library

Copyright © Michael H. C. Baker 2018

ISBN 978-1-78155-710-5

The right of Michael H. C. Baker to be identified as the author of this work has been asserted by him in accordance with the Copyright, Designs and Patents Act 1988.

All rights reserved. No part of this publication may be reproduced, stored in a retrieval system or transmitted in any form or by any means, electronic, mechanical, photocopying, recording or otherwise, without prior permission in writing from Fonthill Media Limited

Typeset in 10.5pt on 13pt Sabon
Printed and bound in England

Acknowledgements

Most of the photographs are by the author, one or two by friends in the Great Western Society, and a number by Brian Morrison, just about the best-known railway photographer of the last sixty years, so famous he has even had a main line locomotive named after him, so I am most grateful for Brian's contributions.

Introduction

There are few places more exciting than a main line terminus and thus it will be easily understood that there would be a particular affection for one encountered at the age of a few months and visited regularly ever since. Paddington is that station, the year of that first visit 1937. Brought up on the Southern Electric, where steam trains were few and far between and then mostly freights hauled by elderly, unnamed tank engines, Paddington offered something utterly different. Those early visits were annual, notwithstanding the wartime exhortations from the age of two to eight to consider if our journeys were 'really necessary'; later, free of parental restraint, the visits became much more frequent. My mother's childhood home was a few miles north of Shrewsbury and we returned there for our annual holidays, staying in the cottage of her favourite sister, Aunt Agnes; she was married to Uncle Frank, the cowman on a large, modern farm, which was part of an estate belonging to the Bibby family of Liverpool shipping fame, and which over several generations gave employment to various members of the family. It is not to be wondered that the Great Western Kings became my favourite engines and chocolate and cream the perfect livery for the carriages they hauled, for it was a King that almost invariably was to be found standing at the head of the dozen or more carriages, out beyond the great arches of Paddington station, ready to depart at ten minutes past the hour for Shrewsbury, stopping at Banbury, Leamington Spa, Birmingham Snow Hill, Wolverhampton Low Level, and Wellington.

In most of those early journeys, finding a seat was rather fraught as the train was always crowded and reservations were not possible. I do not recall ever having to stand, unlike long distance journeys on the Southern where we once had to travel all the way from Waterloo to Southampton in the guard's van, which reeked of fish, but we never managed to find accommodation in my preferred choice, which would have been in one of the then almost new 'Sunshine' carriages. These had big windows and doors only at the end or middle so that once ensconced, one could relax with no intrusions as in the older carriages with a door to each compartment.

The GWR had only adopted this design, no doubt influenced by the LMS and, to a lesser extent, the LNER, in the mid-1930s and more often than not, we occupied a toplight with its distinctive small hammered glass panels above the main ones—not that I had any complaint for the upholstery was comfortable and all GWR carriages in my experience rode smoothly.

We would arrive at Paddington by bus, which stopped in Praed Street. It has to be said that the approach to what is a magnificent station was less than impressive—a rather gloomy, not very wide slope, with a high brick wall on one side and a very much higher office block on the other, down which we made our way and arrived at the Lawn, otherwise known as the concourse. No one seems to know how the Lawn got its name, the assumption being that once, there was a patch of grass there back long before living memory.

What I never realised until many years later was that the tall office block was actually one of the few, and certainly one of the finest, examples of Art Deco architecture in London. It was built in 1934 but, being far more interested in the wonders within the soaring arches at the end of the slope, I never bothered to look up. By the 1940s, the Lawn was a wide open space, well-lit, and always full, not just of bustling people but bustling luggage and parcels trolleys, which were hauled by a fleet of little four-wheel Mercury tractors. They were built in Gloucester, which, of course, was in Great Western territory and perhaps that was why Paddington favoured them. In those days, parcels were big business on the railways and the Mercury drivers were highly skilled, weaving their way with their train of trolleys in tow among the passengers and piles of luggage with never a mishap—at least not in my experience.

Train departures, especially long distance ones, are pure theatre. The Shrewsbury train usually left from platform one. Here was the beating heart of the station; this seemed to add to the drama as though all other activity in the station faded into the background as when the time for departure arrived, doors were slammed, whistles blown, and, slowly and at first, almost imperceptibly, we got under way.

Beside platform one was the main entrance for those arriving by taxi, the booking hall, various shops, the refreshment rooms, and the gentlemen's and ladies lavatories (where, at one time, the fattest cat in London was said to live). Above were various offices, including those that had been occupied by Isambard Kingdom Brunel and Daniel Gooch and whence, many years later, I was able to look out across the platforms in 1979 and see a steam locomotive again, the first for some twelve years, in the shape of No. 5900 *Hinderton Hall* in steam at the buffer stops, having arrived from Didcot to take part in the 125th anniversary celebrations of the station. There were sixteen platforms in all: one to six were for departures, seven to twelve for arrivals, and thirteen to sixteen for suburban and Underground Metropolitan services.

Situated as it was, there was open access to platform one, unlike the other departure platforms—presumably travelling ticket inspectors had to be extra vigilant on all trains leaving it—and it was therefore much favoured by trainspotters who congregated at the country end. There was actually another platform beyond this, serving the parcels business and spotters needed to keep out of the way of the Mercury tractors going to and fro. There was, naturally enough, no public access to this but I did once board a train leaving from it. This was in September 1981 during an open day at Old Oak Common, the huge locomotive and carriage depot serving Paddington. The last built BR steam locomotive, No. 92000 *Evening Star*, was in charge at the western end of the shuttle service with No. 5051 *Drysllwyn Castle* at the other. Old Oak Common was the depot serving Paddington, the largest on the GWR/Western Region and is rare among London area locomotive depots in that it still survives. Strictly speakin,g it is the carriage depot, accessible from the main line by the same junction as the locomotive sheds, which is still with us as the HST depot, but we will consider all this a bit later.

There was also a depot a few hundred yards out of Paddington at Ranelagh, which was actually a servicing point for main line locomotives due to make return journeys to the west, and distinctly unpopular with the surrounding residents living in closely packed flats and tenements where they faced a losing battle on wash day against the effects of smoke and smuts. Ranelagh lasted into the diesel era but is long gone, a parking space where it once was.

In the austerity years of the Second World War, carriages due for overhaul were supposed to lose their glorious chocolate and cream and have it replaced by a sombre all-over brown. However, my recollection is that chocolate and cream was still the livery worn by most corridor carriages, all-over brown being more common on the non-corridor ones employed on the suburban services out of Paddington and around Birmingham. There is plenty of evidence that brown was applied to corridor carriages but no doubt, most never did get around to being repainted in the war years. Certainly from Aunt Agnes's upstairs window, I could see north to west expresses passing a field away and one could always distinguish an express from a stopping train by the former's mix of dark red LMS vehicles and the GWR's chocolate and cream.

The annual journey out of Paddington that must have caused my parents the greatest worry and apprehension was that of 1944. We had survived the Blitz of 1940–41 more or less unscathed, after continuous nights spent either in the cupboard under the stairs or, if the wailing siren had given us time to reach it, in the Anderson shelter at the end of the garden, eventually evacuating ourselves to an abandoned bungalow beside the sea near Bognor Regis. Gradually, the Luftwaffe found targets other than the South London suburbs. Just as we thought the worst was over and Mrs Edwards, headteacher of Rosedene Preparatory School (whose son was still a prisoner of war, having been captured in North Africa), had led us in prayers on D-Day, suddenly flying bombs (doodlebugs) were unleashed. We retreated once more to the shelter listening for what sounded rather like a demented motorcycle to pass overhead or, if the engine cut out, to prepare for the huge 'Crump' as it landed nearby but hopefully not on us. Between fifty and 100 doodlebugs a day hit London at the height of their effectiveness, a fair proportion on Croydon and its surroundings. So once again, Mother and I took ourselves off, to Shropshire, while Granny prepared to go to Poole to stay with Uncle Will at his shoe shop in the high street. Dad stayed behind, working at the NAAFI headquarters at Claygate. Even now, I can recall the relief I felt as our jam-packed train pulled out of Paddington and we headed through the largely unscathed north-west suburbs of Ruislip and into the Chilterns. Even though Cousin Fred survived the Normandy landings, he was tragically killed three days later.

Paddington itself had suffered damage, the most recent some three months earlier on 21 March during what was termed the 'Mini-Blitz', when a last ditch attempt by manned aircraft to wreak havoc on London had petered out but not until many more Londoners had been killed. Shortly after our departure, a flying bomb fell on Paddington station, wrecking the area around platforms six and seven, thankfully with few casualties. There were five bombing incidents in and around the station in all but traffic in and out was relatively little-affected throughout the war.

In the Mass Observation Archive, there is this account by L. B. of Paddington on 14 September 1944:

> My goodness, but it's like Blackpool on Bank Holiday … There are crowds of people everywhere … men and women, and children of all ages and stages. The luggage is piled high on platforms … stacks and stacks of it, trunks and suitcases. Prams, cots, and bicycles in their hundreds. Light and heavy rescue workers of the Civil Defence are working at top pressure to reduce the pile but every incoming train brings its fresh load of luggage.

L. B. goes on to describe some of the passengers:

> The middle aged gentleman immaculately dressed with a walking stick and lemon gloves … the labourer all dressed up in his Sunday best, all with their eyes glued on the indicator … once the train is indicated there was a scramble for the platform.

On 1 July 1944, Mum received a telegram from Dad to say that a flying bomb had landed on the houses backing on to ours. Dad had been at work; Granny was visiting friends nearby and although shocked, she had suffered nothing worse than cuts. Eight houses were totally demolished and thirty severely damaged (including ours, which had its roof blown off and all its windows shattered). Five people were dead. Some days later, another telegram told us that Dad has been transferred to Bournemouth where NAAFI had taken over the Beacon Hotel on the cliff tops and that he had found accommodation for us over a tobacconist shop in the town centre, so we returned.

The journey back to London took much longer than the usual four hours as we were diverted by way of the original route through Oxford, presumably because of what was euphemistically described as an 'incident' on the direct route by way of High Wycombe. It was not a situation where I was in a frame of mind to take much notice of what we were hauled by, not would my mother had let me out of her sight to go and look anyhow. I do remember it was an unusually hot late afternoon when we arrived back in Thornton Heath, staying overnight with friends before we were due to continue our journey to Bournemouth from Waterloo the next day. We were sitting down to tea when suddenly there was the most appalling crash, quite the most terrifying sound I had ever heard, and as we dashed for the indoor

Morrison shelter in the next room, I looked up, quite convinced that I would see the ceiling collapse and the lathes exposed—a common enough sight in Thornton Heath in 1944. Somehow, the house stayed more or less intact; I have never been able to work out just where this particular flying bomb fell, but in all, 145 V1s descended upon Croydon, the greatest number on any London area borough.

The journey to Bournemouth was spent mostly standing in the guard's van, accompanied by the reek of stale fish. It was worth it for we found ourselves living within walking distance of the beach where I made friends with American soldiers on their way to France, and the nephew of General Montgomery, very much the most famous British general of the war, who was staying in a hotel where my mother worked as a cleaner; however, that is another story.

In the steam days, the most ignored features of the main line termini were the tank engines that brought in the empty stock and hauled it out again. Seldom very clean, painted in unlined black, where the colour could be determined at all, without names and often elderly, there was no competition when it came to comparison with the magnificent beasts in charge of the heavily loaded expresses. The pannier tanks that monopolised business at Paddington, though seldom really grubby, and in GWR days were green rather than black, were so commonplace all over the system from the remotest Welsh Valley to just about every siding between Birkenhead, Penzance, and the London suburbs as to be almost anonymous. This was rather an oversight, for if the GWR did not have a patent on the pannier system of storing water, Paddington was certainly the only London terminus where it could be encountered, and the many varieties of stubby, square-faced little engines had tremendous character. The most common of all was the 57xx class of which no fewer than 863 were built between 1929 and 1949. In the 1940s, they had a lion's share of empty stock working in and out of Paddington. There were variations on the 57xx theme, including ten (Nos 9701–10) fitted with condensing apparatus for working over the Metropolitan lines to Smithfield meat market; these were also regular performers on Paddington empty stock workings.

Just before nationalisation, Swindon brought out the first of the 94xxs, which were really tank engine versions of the No. 2251 0-6-0 tender engines and were the first pannier tanks to sport taper boilers. One really has to question the need for them as the 57xxs could cover any duty the 94xxs might perform. Nevertheless, the Western Region embraced the class with enthusiasm and as the 1954 edition of the Ian Allan ABC noted, 'locomotives of this class are still being delivered'. Excellent though they might have been, they were a dreadful waste of money, the last not coming out until October 1956, well into the era of the diesel shunter, with withdrawal of the class beginning three years later. The first ten came out in 1947 and almost all were allocated to Old Oak Common, the class remaining a familiar sight on empty stock workings until the end of steam. The last were taken out of service in a mass cull of the survivors in June, 1965.

Finally, there were the most curious of all the pannier tanks: the ten 15xxs. These broke with tradition in that they had outside cylinders, Walschaert valve gears, and no running boards. Allegedly of 'austerity' specification, they were actually the heaviest GWR 0-6-0Ts. Intended to work in the South Wales docks, they proved much too big for the task and six were sent to Old Oak Common to add yet more variation to empty stock workings.

The only other tank engines regularly seen at Paddington in the period I knew it were the 61xx 2-6-2Ts. They had a near monopoly of the suburban services in and out of the capital from their introduction in 1931 until steam disappeared in 1964. Identical to the 51xxs seen elsewhere on the GWR, apart from increased boiler pressure, the seventy members of the class will forever be associated with the capital as they were also employed on empty stock workings and most were shedded either at Old Oak Common or Southall, the next shed down the line towards Reading.

Come peacetime and in the late 1940s, trains were as crowded as they had been during the war as with full employment, people were better off than ever before, petrol remained rationed, and rail travel was booming. Finding a seat was still far from guaranteed although we always seemed to manage it in the end. It must have been either 1947 or 1948 when I made my only excursion into a clerestory carriage. It seemed to me a poor thing, with a low roof and a gloomy interior and by that date would have been the best part of fifty years old. None, I think, ever received British Railways livery although the last did not disappear from ordinary passenger service until 1953. This was not quite the end—one survived in departmental stock at Old Oak Common at least until 1956, and there are preserved examples.

It was the 1950 visit that brought home to me that the Great Western Railway had gone for good. Awaiting us, not on platform one but on platform three, was a train composed certainly of GWR-built carriages but the entire rake newly repainted in British Railways red and cream, with a blue-painted King at its head. Chocolate and cream would linger on, the last I can recall being in the Birmingham area around 1953 but by then, the first BR-designed carriages—the Mark 1s—were appearing, and by 1955, whole rakes of them formed some Birkenhead expresses (though not entirely, for there never seemed to be enough BR-built refreshment cars to go around, and for several years, indeed into the 1960s, a rake of Mark 1s complete with one, sometimes two, GWR-built refreshment cars was a common sight on expresses at Paddington).

Most remarkable among them were 70-foot-long carriages dating back to pre-1914 days, refurbished and modernised in the 1930s but recognisably of Churchward origin. Some even reassumed simplified versions of their old chocolate and cream livery for from 1956, Swindon was allowed to repaint its named expresses thus; these included the Cambrian Coast Express and the Inter City. A number of new named trains were introduced, just so that chocolate and cream could be seen in many of its old haunts, and why not?

The Inter City had been introduced in 1951, being the 9 a.m. from Paddington to Wolverhampton, returning at 4.25 p.m. By 1963, it had been extended to Chester, leaving Paddington at 8.20 a.m. and returning from Chester at 2.30 p.m. but by then, chocolate and cream had been abolished, replaced by dark red, the Kings all withdrawn, and Western diesel-hydraulics put in charge. After most of the last signs of Western individuality had finally been wiped out, chocolate and cream lingered on individual carriages, dispersed from their once exalted state in a named express and at least one, perhaps more, could be seen working out of Birkenhead on Paddington expresses for almost as long as through trains to Paddington continued, which takes us up to 1967.

The station had survived the war, pretty much intact but increasingly in need of tender, loving care. Victoriana was not a favoured concept, the great arch at Euston station was demolished, and the Great Western Royal Hotel at Paddington station (the very first of the great station hotels built in the nineteenth century) had been messed about in the 1930s by P. A. Culverhouse, the GWR's architect. He certainly knew a thing about Art Deco, but, to quote Steven Brindle writing in *Paddington Station: Its History and Architecture*, '[his] work was a typical instance of the 1930s reaction against Victorian taste, but with hindsight it was very regrettable'.

There were plans in 1952 for a hideous group of high rise tower blocks over the goods station, which never materialised. However, by the late 1960s, attitudes to the nation's glorious Victorian heritage were changing, and in future, it was hoped that any developments at Paddington would be done with care and an appreciation of its nineteenth century splendours: yet vigilance remains the byeword. The Lawn was increased in size to give more circulating space, the tracks being pushed back, the roof was reglazed, with lighter supporting material and twenty years later, 'the fullest and most thorough repair of the roof ever to have been undertaken' occured. Successive improvements meant that light filtered through to all corners, taking advantage of the great roof arches.

The suburban side of Paddington had once been a completely separate station: Bishop's Road, originally jointly operated by the Metropolitan Railway and the GWR. Eventually, in 1933, the name Bishop's Road was dropped and its four platforms became numbers thirteen to sixteen, but they were still not part of a terminus for the tracks continued on into the tunnel and joined with the rest of the Underground network. Of course, most GWR suburban trains did actually terminate here. Those that did continue were handed over to Metropolitan Railway electric locomotives but all this ceased at the beginning of the Second World War. However, the six sets of carriages that had been built for this service in 1920–21, known as the main line and city stock, remained a familiar sight on suburban workings out as far as Oxford until 1957, their capacity, if not their comfort (although they were considerably better than their GNR/LNER contemporaries found at Kings Cross and Broad Street), ensuring that the operating authorities were loth to dispose of them. They were by some margin the last toplights seen in any great number at Paddington. Each set was made up of six carriages, shorter and narrower than normal, in order to negotiate the Underground, and close coupled. Most fortunately, the Great Western Society at Didcot has restored one of the brake thirds so its delights can still be sampled.

Non-corridor carriages were a bit of an acquired taste, something now quite outside the experience of present-day travellers, other than on preserved lines. They were much favoured by the operators of commuters services, who could cram huge numbers into a single train, although much loathed by said customers, for exactly the same reason. The GWR could be said to have catered for the

London commuter rather better than the others of the London Midland and Scottish, the London and North Eastern, and the the Southern Railways, partly because there were less of them, and also because many were rather affluent Thames Side dwellers who expected preferential treatment. Other than the six main line and city sets, the standard formation, until DMUs superceded steam, was a five-carriage train, most of the vehicles being of almost flat-sided Hawksworth design, built between the late 1940s and 1953, although there were also some BR-designed successors, and earlier, slightly more curvaceous Collet-era ones. Painted by British Railways in plain, unlined dark red and without mouldings of any description, they were not the sort of carriages to make the pulses race and they had just about all gone, unmourned, by 1961. This was a great pity for they were what so many people travelled in every day—the most typical perhaps of British railway carriages but not the sort of carriage, with a very few exceptions, that anyone thought to preserve. We are lucky in that the two surviving main line and city examples—one remains unrestored—at Didcot were sent after their days in the London area over to South Wales to carry miners to and from work and thus lasted until 1964, two years after the inaugural meeting of what would become the Great Western Society.

My travels in such carriages were limited as I only occasionally used the suburban side of Paddington station. The RAF, having called me up for National Service on 16 January 1956, was kind enough to send me in April of that year to Credenhill, a few miles west of Hereford, to learn to be a typist, and then to post me, qualified but hardly in the Olympic category of performers, to Abingdon. I like to tell the grandchildren that I was in charge of an Imperial, hoping that they will assume this was a variation on the Lancaster/Halifax/Lysander theme. Either way, both venues were on the Western Region, which was nice. RAF Abingdon managed to do without my services quite frequently at weekends and I would regularly return on weekend leave from Paddington on an express to either Reading or Didcot, and there board a Paddington to Oxford stopping train of non-corridors to Radley where there would be a connecting bus for the camp. My first experience of a BR standard non-corridor carriage was on a stopping train to Didcot returning from an illicit but highly satisfying visit to Swindon Works, in 1954, and in those days, Stratton Park Halt, Shrivenham, Uffington, Challow, Wantage Road, and Steventon were all still open. At Didcot, our train decided to become if not quite an express then certainly a semi-fast to Paddington. I was rather impressed with the hardly luxurious but perfectly comfortable fittings and ride, indeed thought it rather better than the corridor Mark 1s.

By this time, I had begun to take a serious interest in photography, which is not to say the early results using Dad's folding Kodak Brownie (with shutter speeds that claimed to be 1/25th and 1/50th of a second but which in reality seemed to depend on whether or not the camera was in a co-operative mood) were entirely satisfactory, or, to put it another way, much resembled the subject. However, a better camera resulted in better results, which was just as well for I then began to explore the approaches to Paddington, aided sometimes by a very nice Mr Spencer at Paddington, who dispensed permits to visit Old Oak Common Shed.

I also found various lineside venues, such as Royal Oak and Westbourne Park stations, where, of course one could quite legally ply one's trade but also right beside the track at Subway Junction and just east of Old Oak Common, where I was quite definitely trespassing but was never once challenged.

Many of my visits to Subway Junction, some three-quarters of a mile from the platform ends at Paddington, were in the late afternoon or on summer evenings, which was ideal in that departing trains were heading straight into the sun—that is, when it was shining. I used to go through the always open gates of the Crimea coal yard and take up position within sight of Subway Junction signal box beside the track used by pannier tanks and sometimes 61xxs, bringing in the empty stock to form departing expresses. Mostly, I stayed on the down side of the tracks but on a couple of occasions, I rose early in order to photograph the morning rush hour arriving, and the Bristolian departing; this meant carefully picking my way across all the tracks at a particularly busy period, under the watchful eye of the Subway Junction signalman, passing the time of the day with the occasional track worker, and going about my business unchallenged. I blush to think of it now, but the world was a different place then.

Subway Junction got its name from where the Metropolitan Hammersmith line, after leaving Royal Oak station, dived under all the GWR lines and emerged just before passing under the bridge on which the Westbourne Park station buildings were located. From there, it curved into the station platforms before continuing south-westwards past Portobello Road to the terminus at Hammersmith. Immediately opposite the coal yard was the extensive goods depot, which was built on the site of the steam depot, which had closed in the early years of the twentieth century. Serving Paddington since 1855, by the twentieth century, this was no longer fit for purpose, hemmed in as it was on all sides and so was replaced by Old Oak Common in 1906, a mile away. The goods depot, like all the ones in the vicinity of Paddington, went the way of all such establishments, Westbourne Bus Garage being erected on the site, with Westway a continual backdrop right down to Paddington station. It is astonishing to recollect just how many goods depots there were in and around Paddington, although I have to say during daytime, goods trains were few and far between, most of their activities being confined to night time when passengers were safely tucked up in bed (though there were still a few of these, most of them tucked up in sleeping cars).

I never came across any other spotter/photographer/trespasser at this particular location, but it was a different matter at Old Oak Common. Being some distance from any GWR/WR station, I usually approached it on a 630 trolleybus. This was by most measurements the longest regular London trolleybus route and I used to travel all but a couple of its 14.65 miles from West Croydon to just short of what was surely the most peculiar destination on record, 'Near Willesden Junction'. One could also travel to Paddington by trolleybus: the 662 from Sudbury and the 664 from Edgware terminating beside the statue of Sarah Siddons at Paddington Green. Old Oak Common was so near Willesden Junction that one could often hear the hoot of Stanier pacifics, very different from the higher pitched GWR voices. Originally, the GWR directors had planned to share the London and

Birmingham Railways' Euston terminus, and it was only at the last minute that they decided traffic might justify their own establishment, which is why their main line in from the west swerves to the right as it approaches Old Oak Common instead of heading straight on.

The 630 would drop me off at Scrubbs Lane—what a charming title— immediately before passing over the GWR line on its way to 'Near Willesden Junction'. I would cross the road, descend a track, and ensconce myself beside the tracks. Quite often, there would be others there and in preparing this piece, I came across a picture from the mid-1930s and, lo and behold, there are spectators watching the trains go by. Things were clearly much more relaxed; for instance, take a look at one of the finest railway pictures ever taken, by E. R. Wethersett, of the inaugural run of the Silver Jubilee in September 1935 at Potters Bar, and there are spectators—men, women, and children—standing on the low embankment inside the fence. No one ever questioned one's presence at Old Oak Common in the 1950s and 1960s but if you had attempted the same decades later, incarceration in the Tower of London was a possibility, for in 1994, the Eurostar depot was built here. Incidentally, I never did manage to get a train and a trolleybus in the same picture, the best attempt being trolleybus poles disappearing over some buildings in the far distance. This part of London is not what could ever be described as picturesque, unless one was a conniseur of assorted, low rise industrial premises, but as partial compensation, there were some interesting names: Wormwood Scrubs, Mitre Bridge Road, North Pole Junction, and the aforementioned Scrubs Lane, being but four.

I took my first photograph there one July evening in 1955—a surprisingly acceptable one of a condensing pannier tank heading west with a goods train. I ventured into the shed and was delighted to find one of the three surviving Stars, No. 4062 *Malmesbury Abbey*, most unusually coupled to a flat sided Hawksworth tender, preparing to back down to Paddington, and stationed on what was known as the '47 road', the traditional home of those unique, big Churchward 2-8-0s, which specialised in heavy, overnight freights; although almost at the end of their careers and into the Warship diesel era, they were most remarkably put to work— and kept time—on busy summer weekends on expresses to the west of England.

Fittingly, No. 4700 was ahead of the Star. No. 4700 was thirty-six years old, while No. 4062 was just three years younger; that tells you all you need to know about the quality of Churchward's designs as these two veterans were still employed on front line duties. Of other pictures taken at that time of moving trains on the main line, the least said the better.

It was not until I acquired a much better camera in 1957 with vastly quicker shutter speeds, that I could be fairly certain of achieving respectable results. This was just in the nick of time for the first Warship diesel-hydraulics came out of Swindon in 1958, the last Star (No. 4056 *Princess Margaret*) was withdrawn in 1957, and the first true Castle—and not a rebuilt Star—(No. 4091 *Dudley Castle*) was withdrawn at the beginning of 1959. Well before I started taking photographs, I had begun collecting numbers while Stars and, to a lesser extent, Saints, were a familiar feature of the Paddington scene at the beginning of the 1950s.

Although none were allocated to Old Oak Common Stars from Oxford, Bath Road, Bristol, which had no fewer than thirteen, and other sheds ensured their regular appearance in the capital; I seemed to see No. 4021 *British Monarch* of Oxford, in particular on almost every visit, and when the last (*Princess Margaret*) was withdrawn in October 1957, Paddington never seemed quite the same again. My last sight of the *Princess Margaret* had been earlier that year, belting along with a lengthy Paddington to Bristol express west of Slough.

The Newbury Race Trains were always worth looking out for. They were composed exclusively of first-class carriages and dining cars, hauled by specially cleaned Kings and Castles. There was one in particular, the leading vehicle of which was a magnificent 70-foot toplight brake first, No. 8179, dating from 1910; unlike the surviving Churchward-era refreshment cars, in original, unrebuilt condition, this was the only one I ever came across repainted by BR in lined maroon, which lasted until 1961. By that time, it was not only carriages of the Churchward era that were disappearing but later ones too, most expresses being composed of BR Mark 1s, although Collett and Hawksworth vehicles still appeared—sometimes complete rakes of them at busy summer weekends.

The year 1962 saw the mass withdrawal of the Kings, which went straight from express work to the scrapyard with no dying fall on stopping passenger or pick-up goods, unlike many of the last generation of top link express steam locomotives (the Stanier, Bulleid, and ex-LNER pacifics). Although the Castles lasted longer, their days too were numbered and on 11 June, 1965, I photographed No. 7029 *Clun Castle* passing Subway Junction with the last scheduled steam-hauled passenger train out of Paddington.

By then, the Western Region—or was it still, as some insisted, the Great Western Region—was deeply committed to the diesel-hydraulic, rather than the diesel-electric motive power option. The result was some very distinctive designs, some of them little short of a disaster, none of them very long lived. It would be the iconic 'High Speed Train' that would become synonymous with Paddington and its trains to South Wales, Bristol, and the West Country for the next forty years.

Electrification would eventually arrive at Paddington in June 1998, long after the other great London terminals—Marylebone being the one exception—and even then, only for the short branch to Heathrow Airport; main line electrification was still decades away. It was not until October 2017 that the first regular, long-distance electric trains appeared in Paddington, and even then, they operated only as such as far as Maidenhead, the rest of their journey being on diesel power. The trains were the rather fabulous looking Hitachi Class 800 bi-modes, a Japanese design but built in the north-east of England. Very atmospheric as Paddington could be in the steam age, it has to be said that the absence of smoke and steam (and later the fumes from the iconic Western class diesel-hydraulic locomotives) has ensured that the station now looks in better shape, more pristine and cared for, and certainly environmentally better acceptable than ever before.

Above: Carr. This is how I remember Paddington when the great station and my infant self first got together: chocolate-and-cream-painted carriages, smoke and steam rising high into the arched roof, people and luggage everywhere, platform one lined with shops stretching away into the distance beyond the roof where, if there was time, I might be allowed to take a look at our green-painted, copper-capped locomotive. (*Author's collection*)

Below: The photograph shows how accurately Carr had reproduced the Paddington scene. Here, the most famous GWR express to the West Country, the Cornish Riviera, is getting ready for its time-honoured 10.30 a.m. departure time. The empty carriages have been brought in by a 57xx pannier tank shedded at Old Oak Common for just such duties. (*Author's collection*)

Above: Who says trainspotters were invented only by Ian Allan after the Second World War, and who says it was for boys only? I cannot pretend that I have any recollection of No. 6014 *King Henry VII* looking exactly like this at the head of its train on platform one, wearing only the streamlined accoutrements for a matter of months in 1935 as it was before my time, and bits soon began to be removed. The general opinion was that it was all a typical mid-1930s passing fad, epitomised by Hollywood and the Art Deco movement, which certainly suited Nigel Gresley's wonderful, fully streamlined LNER A4 pacifics, but did nothing for *King Henry VII*—a wag once suggested the bulbous front would have been more suitable on No. 6013 *King Henry VIII*. No. 6014 did retain its sloping cab front for the rest of its career. Personally, I would have loved to seen the complete thing, which I thought had real style. (*Mullinger*)

Below: Another picture from rather before my time, this is the Eastbourne Terrace arrival side in 1922. It would have looked just like this fifteen years later, other than changing dress and hairstyles, more modern looking buses, and somewhat more modern looking taxis, although the London taxi has always looked a dozen or more years behind the times. (*Author's collection*)

Above: Eastbourne Terrace looking east (instead of west) in October 2017. Great works are going on at what used to be the arrival side of the station, in connection with Crossrail, due to open at the end of 2018. Otherwise, the actual station buildings are not greatly changed. Those on the opposite side are changed utterly. Is it called Eastbourne simply because it is not Westbourne, a name embedded in the story of the Paddington area? I do not know.

Below: This is the type of bus I would have arrived at Paddington in: one of the late pre-war standard London Transport STL type of AEC Regent, seen at London Bridge, a station much bashed about in the Blitz. (*Author's collection*)

Above: You could also travel to Paddington by trolleybus. London Transport once owned the largest fleet of trolleybuses in the world. This is Paddington Green, which the trolleys circumnavigated in deep snow on their very last day of service on this route, 1 January 1962.

Left: Sitting in the middle of Paddington Green is the statue of Sarah Siddons, 1755–1831. She was quite the most famous actress of the early nineteenth century, was painted by Joshua Reynolds, among others, and gave a Lady Macbeth that had princes grovelling at her feet. She lived at Westbourne Farm and is buried in St Mary's Churchyard, Paddington.

Above: The Metropolitan Railway named its electric locomotives after prominent Londoners. They were used on the lines to Amersham and Chesham, and also hauled GWR trains from Paddington through to the City of London. By a pleasing chance, the only surviving one that is still operational is No. 12 *Sarah Siddons*. I expect you would like to see a picture of it so here it is.

Below: The GWR sign-painting department ensured passengers had very little chance of boarding the wrong train. This handsome late-1930s carriage owes, it has to be admitted, its design concept to the LMS, which pioneered carriages with doors only at the end, enabling each compartment to have its own big-picture window; the GWR called them 'sunshine' carriages. Most Paddington to Birkenhead trains shed several carriages, often including the dining car, at Wolverhampton, where a wheel tapper would be employed to check the remaining vehicles of the train.

Above: Kidderminster toplight. I always hoped to get a seat in such a vehicle but we were much more likely to find ourselves in one of the earlier designs, such as this toplight dating from Edwardian times, or a 1920s vintage bow-ended, Collett-designed carriage with a door to each compartment—not that they were not excellent vehicles, but I did hanker after a sunshine window, which is the norm today.

Below: There are very few examples of Art Deco architecture in London. One of the most notable is the offices on the arrival side of Paddington station. Designed by P. A. Culverhouse, the GWR's architect, and completed in 1935, they are bold and quite splendid. The only problem is that very few passengers ever notice them as they hurry down the slope from Praed Street, unless they should happen to look up.

Above: The Great Western Hotel had little to do with Brunel, being designed by Philip Charles Hardwick, whose father, Philip, was the architect of Euston Station. The design dates from 1851 and was the first really grand station hotel in the UK. For a time in the mid-twentieth century, station hotels fell out of favour—I do not suppose all that smoke and steam had much appeal—but of late, there has been a revival, the wonderfully restored and transformed St Pancras being the prime example. As can be seen in this picture, Paddington's hotel is now part of the Hilton chain, but the 1930s GWR monogram is prominently displayed.

Below: Saint class 4-6-0 No. 2948 *Stackpole Court* about to depart Paddington sometime in the late 1930s. The Saints, along with the Stars, moved the British express locomotive to new heights when Churchward introduced them in the first decade of the twentieth century. By the time Alan Whitehead took this photograph, the Saints had largely been relegated to less demanding duties but could still be relied upon to perform top link duties when asked. The *Stackpole Court* served the GWR and British Railways a few months short of forty years. (*Alan Whitehead*)

Above: No. 4063 *Bath Abbey* heads through Acton with a thirteen-coach West of England express. We can date this picture pretty precisely as the second carriage is one of the Cornish Riviera Centenary wide-bodied vehicles of 1935 vintage—one wonders what it was doing separated from its fellows. Two years later, the *Bath Abbey* was converted to a Castle. Interesting that the Star, which presumably was considered somewhat underpowered, hence its imminent upgrading, seems to be coping with this very lengthy express with a minimum of effort. (*Author's collection*)

Below: An almost new Castle class 4-6-0 No. 5092 *Tresco Abbey* arrives with a lengthy up express *c.* 1939. Successors of the Stars and Saints, the Castle class remained in production from 1923 until early British Railways days, in 1950. Fast and reliable, they were one of the best investments any UK railway company ever made. The *Tresco Abbey* was a rebuild of Star-class No. 4072 of the same name, completed in February 1923. Taken out of service in March 1938, it returned to traffic as a Castle a month later. The last ten Stars were converted to Castles between 1937 and 1940, and although they were not officially classed as rebuilds, they most certainly were for much of the original remained including the frames. (*Author's collection*)

Above: A 1938 scene at Paddington. No. 4926 *Farleigh Hall* ready to depart with the 12.30 p.m. to Weymouth. West of England expresses often included a slip portion for Weymouth, but there was also a regular service of complete trains to the Dorset resort. Not particularly lengthy, this one is composed of modern Collett carriages, complete with a restaurant car. The GWR competed with the Southern Railway for the Weymouth traffic. There was not much difference in times; eventually, in the 1960s, the Southern route out of Waterloo became the winner, the line south from Westbury to Dorchester (where the two routes met) being reduced to single track. *Farleigh Hall*, dates from 1929, and although the Halls were mixed traffic locomotives, they were gradually superceding the Saints on much of their passenger work. (*Mullinger*)

Below: No. 6024 *King Edward I* accelerating out of Paddington. This is a preservation-era picture. The *King Edward I* was fitted with a double chimney in 1957 and thus double chimney and GWR livery never coincided, but, who cares as the King, the pride of the Great Western and the most powerful 4-6-0 ever to grace the metals of the UK, makes quite a splendid spectacle.

Above: Paddington has never handled the volume of suburban traffic to be found at many other London termini, but it is a vital link between towns along the Thames Valley and the West End and City, helped by the London Underground. By the late 1930s, Collett-designed 61xx 2-6-2s were in charge of most of it and would be until dieselisation. However, the much older little Metro tanks had not entirely succumbed to the modern interlopers and here one is passing Old Oak Common, the driver clearly confident of the 0-4-2Ts ability to handle the rake of six, close coupled, non-corridor toplight carriages, dating from around 1920. These carriages, built to reduced dimensions, were worked off the GWR at Subway Junction just outside Paddington, and on to Underground tracks through to the City of London. The outbreak of war brought this service to an end but the high capacity, if not comfort, of this main line and city stock was too valuable to dispense with and these sets lasted until 1957. (*Author's collection*)

Below: Here is a 61xx at the same location, around about the same time hauling much the same sort of train, except that this time, the first carriages are a standard size, four-coach Collett set of non-corridors, with a couple of loose non-corridors bringing up the rear. Note the non-corridor clerestories on the empty carriage road, demonstrating that such veterans could still be seen in Paddington in the 1930s. Note also the small boy in a hat. There was a track that led down from Scrubs Lane over which the 630 trolleybuses passed to the rail side and generations of boys stood there, unchallenged as far as I am aware, to watch the trains go by. (*Author's collection*)

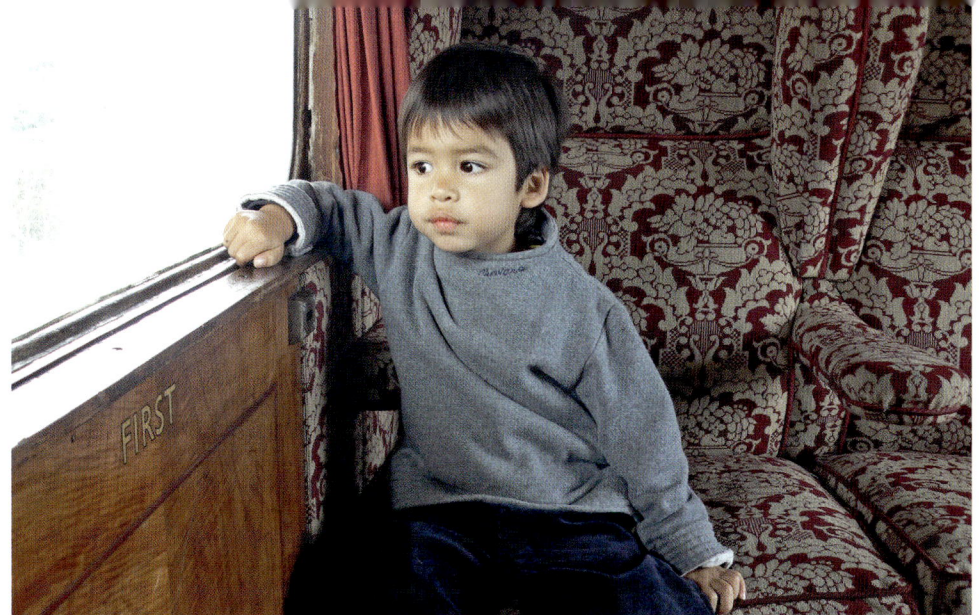

Above: This is my grandson Ben, comfortably ensconced in a preserved late 1930s first-class, sunshine-window carriage. Come the war, forget about the luxuries of first class, we always considered ourselves lucky to get a seat of any sort. As the pannier tank drew the empty stock of our train to a halt at the buffer stops, there would be a mad scramble for the doors, and here, the older door to every compartment carriage was a better bet. The Birmingham and Shrewsbury expresses were generally favoured, even in wartime, with the company's more modern carriages. I can only once recall finding myself in a clerestory roof carriage, which by then would have been getting ready to celebrate its fortieth birthday. It is low roof and dark interior did not impress for in wartime, cleaning clerestory windows was not a priority

Below: Just about enough room on the platform for this vast wartime crowd, with plenty of uniforms about. The carriages represent just about every variety—and the GWR always did go in for variety of carriage style—from late-nineteenth-century clerestory to late 1930s sunshine window. Was their journey 'really necessary'? (*Author's collection*)

Above left: Knowing that war was imminent, the Ministry of Transport had been preparing an evacuation plan for months previously. Put into action, just before war became a reality, on 1 September 1939, no fewer than 1,218,000 people were moved out of London in just four days; half were children and their teachers. Most were taken by bus, tram, trolleybus, and coach to 129 'entraining stations', the majority out in the suburbs to avoid too much congestion at the main line termini; Ealing Broadway, for instance, handled over 100,000 extra passengers. (*Author's collection*)

Above right: The blackout caused great difficulty for railwaymen. Working in goods yards amid shunting engines, almost invariably a pannier tank on the Great Western, had never been the safest of occupations, and it only got worse in the poorly lit wartime conditions, apart from the dangers of bombs raining down, whether incendiary or high explosive. (*Author's collection*)

Opposite above: Here a group of evacuees are seen at Paddington in 1940. Ironically, the carriage they are passing, No. 5428, would later be destroyed in an air raid. Paddington station suffered a number of air raids: the passenger station seven times, the goods station four. The Eastbourne Terrace buildings, on the arrival side, were hit leaving a gap which persisted well into the post-war years, and tracks were destroyed when bombs came through the roof but, as happened all over London, repairs were carried out in a remarkably short time and soon it was, 'business as usual'. I can remember vividly the feeling of relief as our Shrewsbury bound train pulled out of the station in the summer of 1944, when, shortly after the D-Day landings, the first V1 flying bombs (doodlebugs) descended on London and, in particular, on the houses at the bottom of our garden, removing much of the roof and all the windows in our house. We were headed for the rural fastness of Shropshire, the last bit of the journey to Hadnall, first station out of Shrewsbury, courtesy of the LMS and quite likely, even in a stopping train, in a carriage with seats arranged around a table and illuminated by big, sunshine-type windows. (*Author's collection*)

Below: Some 320 evacuees seen on 1 September 1939 arriving from West Ham at Chipping Norton. The next day, two more trains—one the longest ever seen on this branch line—brought in 1,100 more evacuees. Experience of evacuation varied enormously, from those who were desperately homesick, and might be exploited as cheap, unpaid labour, to those who delighted in rural life and looked back on their time in the lush Oxfordshire countryside with great affection. (*Author's collection*)

Above: Locomotive construction did not cease entirely during the war, but it was inevitably reduced and the Big Four co-operated so that, for instance, Swindon turned out a number of LMS-designed Stanier—a Swindon-trained man—8F 2-8-0s. Swindon's first brand-new design was the County class 4-6-0. No. 1000 *County of Middlesex* was completed in August 1945. Very much in the GWR tradition, it nevertheless incorporated variations, not least, plate frames, a new standard No. 15 boiler with the very high pressure of 280 lb based on that of the LMS 2-8-0s, and one long splasher rather than individual ones. The GWR publicity machine gave the impression that the Counties were an improved two-cylinder version of the Castles, but it did not quite work out like that. Initally, eight of the thirty members of the class were allocated to Old Oak Common and seven to Bristol, but the hammer blow of these most powerful of the company's two-cylinder 4-6-0s caused problems, and steaming was not at first entirely satisfactory. This is No. 1017 *County of Hereford*, with a Paddington to Birmingham, Shrewsbury, and Birkenhead express passing over the water troughs at Ruislip in 1947. (*Author's collection*)

Below: The railways of the United Kingdom were nationalised in 1948, bringing to an end the 123-year separate existence of the Great Western Railway. No. 5032 *Usk Castle* is seen about to depart with the very first Western Region train out of Paddington at 12.05 a.m. on 1 January 1948. (*John Lucking*)

Above: For a short while after nationalisation, no identification was applied to Swindon overhauled locomotives. No. 6016 *King Edward V* is near Gerrards Cross with an up Birkenhead to Paddington express sometime in either late 1948 or early 1949. The locomotive has just been repainted in the Caledonian blue, reserved for the most powerful express passenger engines. The leading carriage would appear to be in the new British Railways cream, the rest still in GWR chocolate and cream. (*Brian Morrison*)

Below: Three Kings have been preserved. No. 6023 *King Edward II*, after spending many years in Barry scrapyard, was rescued, brought to Didcot, and is seen there restored to its original, single-chimney condition. It has also been repainted in British Railways blue. Although a short-lived livery, on account of its tendency to fade, this shows just how splendid it looked, and advances in paint technology in the intervening years will ensure that its appearance remains pristine. The leading carriage is painted in the dark red livery, which was adopted by the GWR in the war years, although not all received it.

Above: Paddington is unique among the London termini in that it shares it surface platforms with the Underground. Here, the Red Dragon is arriving from South Wales behind Britannia 4-6-2 No. 70021 *Morning Star* while a Hammersmith-bound train is departing. Despite building the very first British pacific, No. 111 *The Great Bear* in 1908, the GWR subsequently eschewed this wheel arrangement and when a batch of the 1951 vintage BR-standard Britannias was allocated to the Western Region, some going to Old Oak Common depot; they were not received with wild adulation. That probably says more about entrenched GWR attitudes than any faults in the locomotives. Never intended to replace the Kings, being in the same power class as the Castle 4-6-0s, these handsome machines eventually settled at Cardiff Canton depot whence they worked with unspectacular efficiency until moved to the London Midland Region as steam declined. The Underground train is of the highly distinctive, flare-sided stock introduced at the end of 1930s and worked over the Metropolitan, District, and Circle lines from 1937 to 1981.

Below: There had been an Inner Circle line Underground station at Paddington since the 1860s, worked by steam for some forty years. This is an illustration from a children's book of my father's depicting, pretty accurately, an Inner Circle line train in the 1890s. The line from Paddington to Farringdon and Moorgate was the very first Underground railway in the world and such was the GWR's interest in it that it was initially worked by Broad Gauge rolling stock. (*Author's collection*)

Above: The Underground Circle line station in 2015, although, as can be seen, it is only just below the surface and has a handsome curved roof to let in the daylight. It used to look very gloomy and neglected but has recently been given a makeover, as has the entire station—a great improvement. The train is the latest 'S' stock, built at Derby, the first units entering service in 2010. Costing a total of £1.5 billion, production continued until 2017. They have air conditioning and wide connections between carriages giving the impression of one continuous, sinuous vehicle. My earliest recollections of travelling on the Underground were in wooden-bodied carriages and I remember watching, with much apprehension, one of the doors gradually sliding open as we rattled through the tunnels, revealing the opposite track and the exposed Hornby Dublo type central electrified rail. I found this so disturbing that for ages, or it seemed like ages, afterwards, I insisted that we travel to Paddington by bus rather than Underground.

Below: The huge goods station was situated on the up side of the passenger station, its wall forming the background to many pictures of passenger trains arriving. However, not all goods trains terminated here for almost until the end of the steam era some passed through the suburban station and continued on, down the Metropolitan tracks to Smithfield Meat Market. Here, one of the group of ten 57xx-class pannier tanks, fitted with condensing apparatus for this task, is passing the approach to the goods depot with a train of insulated meat vans in the immediate pre-war era. The expressions on the face of casual travellers standing on the platform of a station between Paddington and Smithfield when a Smithfield-bound train came puffing were a sight to behold.

Above: An aerial view looking down on Paddington with the passenger station at the bottom left and the goods station top right. Possibly taken from a GWR airship, although if the company ever owned such a means of transportation, it has escaped my notice. (*Author's collection*)

Below: Bishop's Bridge suburban and Underground station was once regarded as a separate establishment from Paddington main line station and this footbridge leading to it is a reminder of those days.

Above: First Underground station out of Paddington on the Hammersmith line is Royal Oak, although GWR stopping trains also called there until 1934. It is visible across the tracks beyond pannier tank No. 8754. Opposite Royal Oak was Ranelagh depot. No locomotives were allocated there, its function being to provide servicing for those that needed a quick turn around and had not got time to get to and from Old Oak Common. Inevitably, it was a noisy place and quite honestly, it must have been hell sometimes for the inhabitants of the tenements surrounding it. Two railwaymen take a break alongside Ranelagh while No. 8754, on duty No. 5 from Old Oak Common depot, approaches with empty stock for a departing express, *c.* 1959. (*Brian Morrison*)

Below: A westbound train—the indicator has got it wrong, this is not the Circle line—approaching Royal Oak having just dived under the Western main lines, in 2015. This is a 'D' stock train, which operated these lines from 1980 to 2017. To the right, the waste ground is being prepared for Cross Rail, the biggest civil engineering work in the western world and, it might be argued, the final culmination of the GWR's long-cherished plans to expand into the City of London.

Above: This is where the Underground tracks emerge, beside the long-vanished Crimea yard, where coal wagons can be seen. A June 1959 picture with No. 6866, *Morfa Grange* accelerating the 7.30 p.m. Paddington to Oxford and Wolverhampton train, composed entirely of GWR-design carriages, the fourth vehicle being a 70-foot long Edwardian-era dining car refurbished in the 1930s. Behind the Grange, on the up side is a goods depot; until the turn of the century, this had been Westbourne Locomotive Depot. Old Oak Common replaced it.

Below: Both the Underground and the GWR had stations at Westbourne Park. The GWR one opened in 1871 and closed in 1992, which was rather annoying for it had provided an excellent vantage point for photography, but I do not suppose this was taken into consideration, and was not surprising given that in its later years, it was poorly patronised. Two D-stock trains are occupying the station on their way to and from Hammersmith. By this date, a good deal more red paint and a certain amount of blue had been applied—an improvement on their original bland colour scheme.

Above: A 61xx 2-6-2T is arriving at Westbourne Park, the last station before Paddington, with an all stations stopping train from Reading in April 1956. The six carriages are close coupled, Churchward-era main line and city toplight vehicles, dating from 1921 and built especially to be hauled beyond Paddington over the Circle line Underground tracks to the City, which they did until the outbreak of the Second World War. Although they were then confined to the GWR network, they were so valued for their high capacity that they lasted until the late 1950s, and even they were not quite done with for some were sent to South Wales to take miners to and from work. One has been beautifully restored and can be ridden in at Didcot Rail Centre.

Below: Passengers on a city-bound train from Hammersmith at Westbourne Park station.

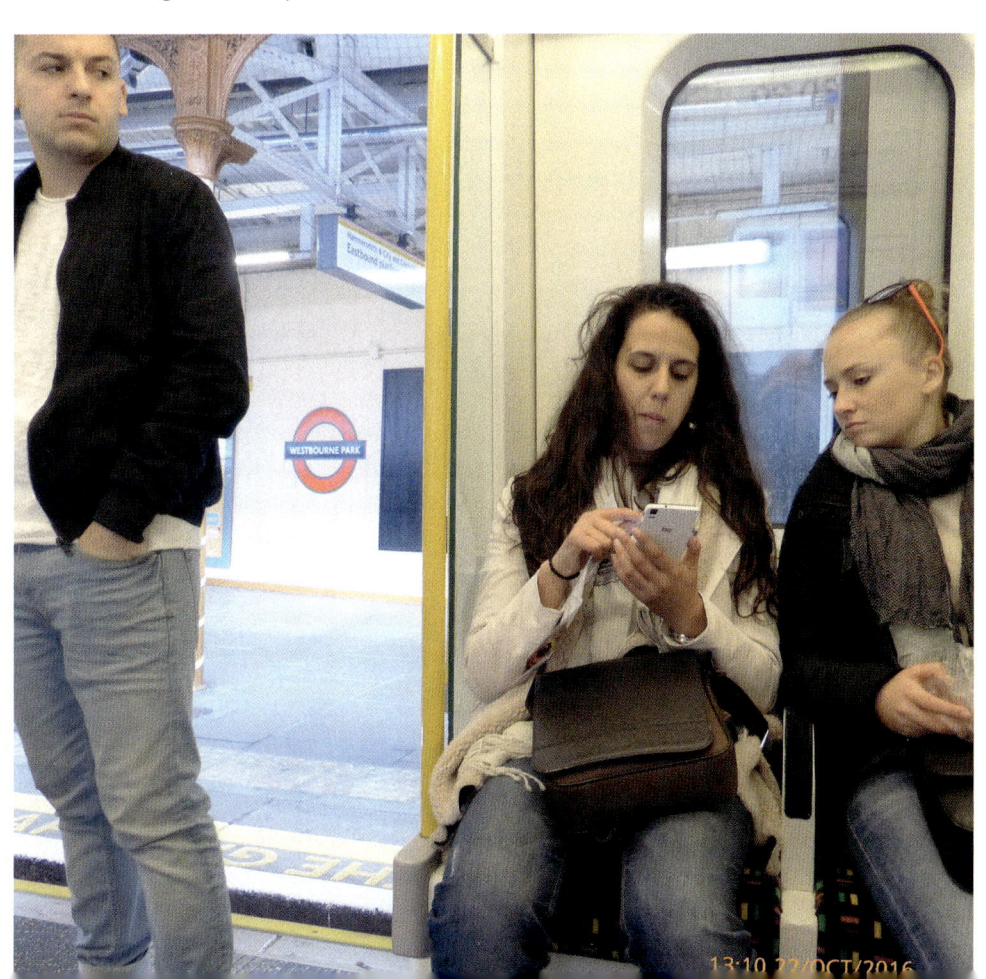

Above: An up Birkenhead express drifts, on time, through Westbourne Park as No. 6008 *King James II* slows with its twelve-carriage train on the approach to Paddington. The Kings were seldom turned out in anything but immaculate condition and the *King James II* is not letting the side down. I do not suppose the terraces in Elkstone Road backing on to the track were the best place to hang your washing, just visible above No. 6008's boiler, not that you would have had much choice. The Victorian terraced houses are, like the *King James II* (both the locomotive and the Stuart monarch, come to think of it), long gone. By this date, BR Mark 1 carriages formed the bulk of expresses in and out of Paddington, although it looks like there are some GWR-era ones at the rear. The train is passing Portobello Junction, where Paddington goods station lines diverged, beyond that the bridge carrying Golborne Road over the tracks, while the train is about to pass under the Great Western Road bridge on which stands the booking office for Westbourne Park station.

Below: One of the things I remember most vividly about the Paddington scene was the small tractors hauling long lines of wagons piled high with luggage, weaving their way in and out of the passengers and porters. They are still there, at least their modern equivalents are, moving stuff around the station.

40

Above: The diesel era did not really begin at Paddington until the late 1950s but the two GWR-designed diesel parcel cars, which spent their time motoring in and out of the station on regular runs out into the suburbs, were forerunners. Here, No. 34, dating from 1941, awaits its next assignment at the long parcels platform, really an extension of platform one. The GWR diesel railcars, introduced in 1934, were truly revolutionary, heralding the universal introduction of the diesel multiple unit by British Railways in the 1950s. The passenger cars did not normally work into Paddington, although they appeared on occasions. The nearest they normally reached was Southall, which was also the home of the two parcel cars. Southall was where the factory of AEC, builders both of London buses and the GWR railcars, was situated. (*Brian Morrison*)

Below: One wonders just how 'express' this parcel delivery would have been in the 1930s, although, to give the horse his due, he might not have been all that much slower than motor vehicles on short runs in congested central London. Many thousands of horses passed into British Railways care in 1948, although all had gone by the of the 1950s. (*Author's collection*)

Above: There remained some parcel work for steam and one of the early 57xx pannier tanks, No. 7791, is passing Acton with a siphon 'G', originally built for milk traffic, and an LMS passenger full brake van. The Western Region seemed very partial to borrowing ex-LMS carriages whenever the opportunity arose. (*Brian Morrison*)

Below: If you enter Paddington main line station by way of the Circle line, you arrive here, at the Lawn. Presumably, deep in the mists of time, there must have been a grass-covered space here, but no record of it would seem to exist. To the left is the entrance down the slope from Praed Street. Always quite spacious, to the right, there used to be, inside a glass case, a very large and very detailed model of a King-class engine and a late 1930s Collett design carriage upon which I would gaze, confirming my long-held belief that the prototypes were the finest examples engineering genius could produce. The Lawn was redesigned in the year 2001, giving more circulating space. I am sure the model still exists but I do not know where.

This is the approach from Praed Street to the station, leading to what used to be the arrival platforms. The section of roof straight ahead is known as 'Span Four', which was added in 1913–15 and very carefully designed to blend in with the original three spans, the sixty-two ribs lining up with those of the Brunel roof. It was refurbished in 2009–2011, and made lighter, a necessary improvement, with due notice being taken of its Great Western Railway ancestry, a welcome contrast to the opinion of one bright young management spark whom I interviewed in the early 1970s who told me the station was 'no longer fit for purpose' and should be bulldozed and replaced. This was not the first, but hopefully the last time this magnificent, historic structure had been under threat. For a while from the 1930s to the 1960s, labelling something as 'Victorian' was generally regarded as a condemnation, hence the destruction of the Euston Arch, although I am not sure the rest of that station was any great loss. St Pancras station and hotel, which is, in the author's opinion, the finest building in London, was in real danger in the 1960s, but John Betjeman led the fight for its retention. The tide turned—the astonishingly creative notion to spare no expense in making it the terminus of Eurostar was a stroke of genius; Victoriana is back in favour to which statues of Brunel and Betjeman attest.

Isambard Kingdom Brunel's statue at Paddington Station. It serves its purpose but does not quite have the 'oomph' that Brunel himself exuded.

Left: Very nearly as famous, certainly among the younger generation, is Paddington Bear. The creation of that lovely children's author, Michael Bond, the bear in question is a native of Peru who had to migrate to the UK when his Aunt Lucy found it necessary to move into a retired bear's home. Her nephew was found on Paddington station by the Brown family, with whom he goes to live nearby and shares many adventures, quite a few of them involving marmalade sandwiches. Like Brunel, Paddington Bear has his statue at the station but, again, it was not really possible to convey the fluffieness of a South Amercan bear in a hard substance, so how about grandaughter Katy with her Paddington instead? Paddington (not Katy's one) has already starred in a full length feature film and, as I write, its sequel has just gone on general release.

Below: No. 1500, representative of a rather unique variety of pannier tank, backing out of platform one after the train it has brought in has departed. There were just ten No. 1500s and they differed from the standard variety in having outside cylinders and Walschaerts valve gear. They came out in early British Railways days and were originally intended to work in the South Wales docks. However, their wheelbase proved too long so the majority were transferred to Old Oak Common and they spent most of their careers hauling empty stock in and out of Paddington. That there were ever only ten of the class and that they proved unsuitable for their intended duties suggests that someone in the Swindon drawing office had rather miscalculated.

Above: The entrance to Old Oak Common depot, the largest on the GWR/Western Region, looking eastwards towards the main line. Colour light signals replaced semaphores on the main line in the 1930s, but the semaphores were still to be seen in profusion protecting the depot into the 1970s. At least ten are in view here.

Below: No. 4062 *Malmesbury Abbey* at Old Oak Common depot, July 1955. This grainy picture was the best my primitive camera could manage on such an evening. Before the Castles arrived in 1923, the Stars were literally the stars of Old Oak Common but by this date, there were just three left and so were a rare sight in London. The *Malmesbury Abbey* is unusually paired with a flat-sided post-war Hawksworth tender. Withdrawn in November 1956, it left No. 4061 *Glastonbury Abbey*, which went four months later, and No. 4056 *Princess Margaret*, taken out of service in October 1957, plus the preserved No. 4003 *Lode Star*. Next to it is an elderly clerestory carriage, demoted to departmental duties but externally complete. The last Saint was withdrawn in October 1953, although the Great Western Society has a replica nearly complete. With the disappearance of the last Churchward 4-6-0s, and their windowless cab, something distinctive had gone from the Paddington scene.

Above: However, the Paddington area continued to regularly see an example of an equally impressive Churchward design for several more years. Taken on the same evening and standing on what was always known as the '47 road' is the pioneer No. 4700, one of nine big 2-8-0s of 1919. These were built specifically to haul the long distance, overnight fitted freight trains, but with their 5-foot 8-inch driving wheels, they were also capable of passenger work, and as we shall see elsewhere in these pages, even into the diesel era they were rostered on summer Saturdays to take charge of West of England expresses.

Below: No one could possibly doubt who was the star of Old Oak Common from 1927 until the end of steam. Here is No. 6000 *King George V*, in all its glory, posing at the depot on 5 May 1959. Built in 1927, declared to be the most powerful locomotive in the United Kingdom, he was sent later that year across the Atlantic to the centenary celebrations of the Baltimore and Ohio Railroad, where he was awarded a bell and gold medals, which he has displayed ever since. Fitted with a double chimney in December 1956, he entered preservation in 1962. We will follow its subsequent history in later pages.

Above: Adjoining Old Oak Common locomotive shed was the large carriage depot. Here we see No. 9118, another pretty special vehicle. The GWR, unlike the Southern and the LNER, wanted little to do with Pullmans. The GWR did, briefly, venture into an agreement with the Pullman Company to run the Torbay Pullman Ltd in 1929 but this was not very successful and was soon withdrawn. However, Swindon decided it could go one better and in 1931 built eight Super, or Ocean Saloons, taking advantage of the extra width the Broad Gauge legacy allowed. Utterly magnificent, equipped with deep-cushioned armchairs, they were used primarily on the boat trains between Plymouth Millbay and Paddington, the patrons, apart from paying the first class fare, being charged another ten shillings for the privilege. Latterly, they might appear at any special event and although their withdrawal coincided with the end of steam, five have been preserved. As can be seen, No. 9118, originally named *Princess Elizabeth*, never lost its chocolate and cream livery and in 1967 moved to the Didcot Railway centre where it still lives. It is a late Churchward era all first non-corridor carriage, used to convey businessmen from their affluent Thames Valley to their offices in central London.

Below: Meanwhile, out of the main line on 21 March 1959 in the everyday, unglamorous commuting world, 2-6-2T No. 6164 comes bustling along the down main line with a five-coach train of post-war Hawksworth-era non-corridor carriages, mostly built in the very early British Railways days. They were plain, painted in unrelieved dark red but were nevertheless a good deal more comfortable than the quad arts of Kings Cross and Liverpool Street, and the various wooden bodied and early 'pack 'em in' steel-sided Bulleid electric multiple units of the Southern termini.

Above: GWR pannier tank locomotives were nothing if not versatile. They were usually found on empty stock workings in and out of Paddington, but as likely as not, one would turn up during the rush hour as a substitute for 61xx, which had been reluctant to get out of bed, as here where N9710 has no trouble with five GWR design non-corridor carriages approaching journey's end on a bright summer morning, 2 June 1961.

Below: Great Western express engines had been designed to burn the best Welsh coal but this was not always available post-war and to restore, and maybe even improve the steaming qualities of the four cylinder express engines, four row superheaters and double chimneys began to be fitted to the Castle class in 1956, although not all received them. This is No. 4090 *Dorchester Castle*, the second to be so equipped in July, with a relief to the Cornish Riviera accelerating to the west past the inevitable small boy watching the spectacle, 4 April 1958.

Above: A rare sight—two Kings passing, one in charge of the down Cornish Riviera, the other climbing the empty carriage road from Old Oak Common depot with empty stock. The main attraction at Old Oak Common was the down Cornish Riviera Express passing just after 10.30 a.m. The Bristolian may have been faster but nothing could compare with the Western's most famous train, which had run since 1904, made up to a dozen carriages, hauled by an immaculate King. In 1956, British Railways announced that named expresses on the Western could again assume a chocolate and cream livery. There was a proliferation of these and, on 11 June 1956, the Cornish Riviera Express joined their ranks. The carriages were new BR Mark 1s, except for the restaurant cars, which were Collett-era 1930s vintage examples; some 70-foot-long Dreadnoughts from Edwardian times also appeared in chocolate and cream in named expresses. Here, on 4 April 1958, No. 6029 *King Edward VIII* has charge. No. 6029 was officially the newest King, being completed in August 1930, but No. 6007 was a newly built replacement in March 1936, the original badly damaged in an accident at Shrivenham that January.

Below: Against the background of Kensington Gas Works condensing pannier tank No. 9707 comes hurrying down the down slow line at Old Oak Common with a short goods, no doubt anxious to keep out of the way of the passenger traffic on a July evening in 1955. As the evening wore on, goods traffic will become plentiful as the passenger business declines. Apart from the huge Paddington goods depot, there were several other yards between the terminus and Old Oak Common in those days, to say nothing of the proliferation of suburban goods yards out to the west in the Reading direction and to the north west on the High Wycombe line.

Above: However, freight might be seen during the daytime, but it was pretty unusual for two freight trains to appear at the same time. This was the scene on a sunny morning on 22 March 1958. Churchward Mogul 6313 from Didcot depot has just emerged from overhaul at Swindon and looks resplendent in lined green livery; it never wore anything quite so grand in GWR days. It was completed on 20 January 1921. It is reversing its short train into the yards at Old Oak Common while in the distance, proceeding along the down main line, is another short freight.

Below: A short while later things got even more exciting when none other than No. 6000 *King George V* came slowly into view and drew to a halt just beyond the Scrubs Lane Bridge. He had charge of the first train of the day from Penzance, which was certainly not scheduled to stop at this particular location, even if it did give the lineside spotters a unique opportunity to examine the Western's pride and joy at close quarters. The guard alighted and other railwaymen appeared, their attention focused around the nether regions of the last carriage. After much discussion the guard came trotting up to King George's cab, more conversation followed, the guard trotted back whence he had come, and No. 6000 gave an impatient whistle before resuming the interrupted journey to the capital. It will be noted that 'pride and joy' of the Western or not, on this occasion, he looks far from pristine and in need of some tender, loving care.

Above: We will return to Old Oak Common later but having metaphorically taken the opportunity to jump aboard train No. 6000, we will head back to Paddington. Behind us is a thirteen-coach train composed entirely of excursion stock, the leading one a bow-ended saloon of the late 1920s, the remainder 1935 vintage, open, sunshine-window carriages, the entire train, apart from the first two, still in the first BR red and cream livery. The locomotive is No. 5067 *St Fagans Castle* of July 1937. Just visible in the top right hand corner are the poles of a 630 trolleybus. I never did manage to persuade a trolleybus to cross the bridge while a train was passing beneath.

Below: I would regularly use the 630 on my expeditions to Old Oak Common. For most of its existence it bore the peculiar, if accurate destination of 'Near Willesden Junction'. There is a link with the GWR in this for at one time, it was intended that the GWR would share the London and Birmingham Railway's terminus at Euston and would join their line in to the capital at Willesden Junction. Indeed, Willesden Junction remained the nearest station to Old Oak Common shed and I used it if I was not going by 630 trolleybus or BSA Bantam. Here we see No. 452, of Leyland manufacture, about to begin its long journey to 'Near Willesden Junction' at West Croydon in August 1954.

Above: The route that passed the actual entrance to Old Oak Common depot was the 666. Once, it would have been the 66 tram. Trolleybus 232 is heading along Old Oak Lane, having just navigated the bridge spanning the tracks above Willesden Junction station, on 16 September 1958. Note the railway men heading home from Old Oak Common depot past terrace houses, in which many railway employees and their families lived.

Below: Churchward Mogul 5330 in fully lined out green livery inside one of the Old Oak Common roundhouses, 6 September 1958. Moguls had not been shedded at Old Oak Common for many years when this picture was taken but No. 5330 was a Didcot engine and 2-6-0s from that depot were regular visitors to London. It was in January 1957 that fully lined-out green livery began to be applied to the class and, judging by No. 5330's excellent condition, it is probably not long out of works. It survived until June 1964, a working life of forty-seven years, the last but two survivor of the 53xx series.

Above: There was always an interesting collection of motive power assembled outside the Factory Repair Shop at Old Oak Common awaiting attention. Note the traverser. On 6 September 1958, Churchward mogul No. 7309 and No. 5040 *Stokesay Castle* are prominent with, among others, a County, a 61xx, a 9F 2-10-0, and a King lining up behind.

Below: A fascinating experiment that turned out to be a dead end but engendered vast interest was No. 18000, a Swiss-built gas turbine locomotive, ordered by the GWR from Brown Boveri and delivered in 1949. It is seen passing Old Oak Common on 13 June 1957 with a fairly lightweight express from Bristol. Referred to in parts of the national express as the 'Jet Engined Locomotive', it was noisy, heavy on fuel and not very reliable—a bold experiment all the same. It was withdrawn in 1960, returned to Switzerland, and after all sorts of vicissitudes, came back to the UK, minus its power unit, and has become yet another Didcot Railway centre resident.

Above: Old Oak Common, 4 March 1958. No. 6012 *King Edward VI* will shortly swing to the north-west just beyond Old Oak Common depot at North Acton Junction and head through Park Royal and Greenford on its way to the West Midlands, the destination being Shrewsbury. Hauling no fewer than thirteen carriages, all of GWR origin, other than one LMS interloper, there would seem to be no restaurant car. Although tough on the passengers, many (like our family) would consider such a facility a needless expense and would come fully equipped with packets of home-constructed sandwiches and Thermos flasks.

Below: No. 6158, one of the ever present 61xxs, has been promoted to a starring role complete with express headlamps and eight GWR-design corridor carriages on 4 April 1958. This is almost certainly a Paddington to Reading, Didcot and Oxford semi-fast, stopping only at certain stations.

Above: No. 6142, 2-6-2T of Old Oak Common shed, has come to a halt on the down main line with its train of ten GWR-design empty corridor carriages, 7 April 1958. With the guidance of a railwayman standing beside the train and watched over by the inevitable boy trainspotters, complete with bikes, it is shunting them into Barlby Road carriage depot. One would not have thought this inevitably drawn-out procedure would have been much welcomed during a busy holiday period.

Below: Another somewhat unexpected sight at Old Common, No. 6835 *Eastham Grange* on 4 March 1958, with a West of England express. Unexpected because the Grange 4-6-0s, with their 5-foot 8-inch driving wheels, were relatively unusual in the London area, certainly compared with the 6-foot Halls, and exceptionally rare on West of England expresses. The *Eastham Grange*'s home was St Phillips Marsh, Bristol, which tended to be inhabited by freight and mixed traffic engines, Bath Road being where the Castles, and, occasionally, Kings lived. All of the *Eastham Grange*'s eight carriages are of Great Western origin, the train being an Easter holiday extra.

Above: It was common practice to provide top link express passenger locomotives on certain tightly timed commuter services along the Thames Valley and here, on 18 April 1960, the penultimate Castle, the immaculate No. 7036 *Taunton Castle* of Old Oak Common depot, heads a mixed rake of corridor and non-corridor carriages on an up Didcot train through Subway Junction as the terminus comes into sight.

Below: A real end-of-era scene at Subway Junction on 12 August 1961. The Britannia pacifics received a mixed reception from WR crews when the first were delivered in 1951, although this probably says more about entrenched GWR attitudes than any deficiencies in these handsome 4-6-2s. Eventually, they found a welcome at Cardiff Canton depot, which is where No. 70016 *Ariel* is based. The carriages are all elderly Colletts dating from the 1920s and early 1930s, apart from two LMS interlopers, and all will be passing to the scrapheap when the summer is over.

Above: The Blue Pullman DMUs were introduced in 1960 on the London Midland Region and were later transferred to the Western from which they were withdrawn in 1973. From time to time, they had to be replaced by a rake of locomotive-hauled Pullmans. This is one such occasion, with a very mixed rake of elderly Pullman cars hauled by the pioneer Western diesel-hydraulic locomotive No. 1000 *Western Enterprise*.

Below: No. 5098 *Clifford Castle*, the first post-war member of its class, completed at Swindon in May 1946, does its best to impress the photographer with its immaculate condition, plenty of smoke, and a rake of chocolate and cream BR Mark 1 carriages, except for the fourth vehicle, a 1930s Collet restaurant car, also in chocolate and cream, as of days of yore, all on a bright sunny day, as he wastes no time heading for the Principality on 7 August 1961. I suppose you could argue that the Red Dragon ought to be composed of red carriages, which would come soon enough when the brief, glorious revival of chocolate and cream would come to an end.

Above: Modifications, including fitting a revised double chimney, turned the two-cylinder 'Improved Modified Hall' counties from being a bit of an enigma into a highly successful passenger locomotive. Most of their careers was spent in the hilly regions of Cornwall and the north to west main line between South Wales, Shrewsbury and Chester, but they could still be seen at Paddington and here, No. 1011 *County of Cheshire* heads into the western sun past Subway Junction with the 7.15 p.m. express to Bristol, 3 June 1960.

Below: The Bristolian, Britain's fastest train, hauled by 5085 *Evesham Abbey*, glides past Subway Junction, dead on time, 3 June 1959. A few days later, Warship diesel-hydraulics took over. Evesham Abbey was a rebuild of a Star of the same name, built in December 1922. Other railways would certainly have called No. 5085 a rebuild, for it contained substantial parts of the Star, including the frames and it says much for Swindon's quality of workmanship that a locomotive approaching its thirty-seventh year could be entrusted for such a prestigious duty.

Above: D805 *Benbow* approaching Wootton Bassett with the up Bristolian. Its schedule is still 105 minutes, as it was for steam, the load still seven carriages including a GWR-built twelve-wheel buffet car. The Warships looked a good deal more stylish than other first generation main line diesels. Although the power units were built in Germany, the locomotive itself was the work of Ruari McLean of Design Associates.

Below: Heading west past Subway Junction is a double-chimney Castle, No. 7019 *Fowey Castle* in charge of a Newbury Race Special. These workings were rather special as they were always in the care of a highly polished Old Oak Common Castle or King and the train was composed entirely of first-class carriages. The date is 4 March 1961; note that thirteen years after nationalisation, the carriages are all of GWR origin, the leading being the most notable. It is a 70-foot-long toplight brake first, No. 8178, one of three built in September 1910 for the Fishguard boat train. By this date, the toplight carriage had virtually disappeared and this was one of the few ordinary ones in unrebuilt condition, perhaps the only one to be repainted by British Railways in its dark red livery. This was an approximation of the livery it first wore, for by 1910, the traditional chocolate and cream had been superceded, although it would be restored after 1918.

Above: Subway Junction, 18 April 1960. Pannier tank No. 9707 has charge of the empty stock, all dark red BR Mark 1s, which it has brought in from Old Oak Common and which will form an express out of Paddington. Westbourne Park bus garage and Westway now fill the space occupied by the goods depot on the other side of the tracks.

Below: We have seen that pannier tank could happily substitute for 61xxs on suburban passenger duties. Just as frequently, 61xxs would return the compliment and take up employment on empty stock work in and out of Paddington. Here, on 7 July 1961 at Subway Junction, No. 6162 heads for the terminus while No. 7024 *Powis Castle* is pulling out with an express composed of GWR-design stock.

Paddington comes into sight as No. 6023 *King Edward II* passes Subway Junction on 18 April 1960 with an up Wolverhampton and Birmingham express. In the distance, rounding the bend, to the right of the two rakes of suburban carriages in the sidings, a down express can just be seen approaching. No. 6023's first two carriages are of GWR design although, as best I can recall, the rest were BR Mark 1s. The *King Edward II*, withdrawn in 1962, spent time in Woodhams scrapyard on Barry Island before being rescued and eventually brought to the Didcot Railway Centre for restoration.

No. 5026 *Criccieth Castle* arriving at Paddington, 20 March 1958. Despite carrying express headlamps, the first three carriages, and pretty certainly, the remainder are all non-corridor, the first being a bulbous-sided brake second-class carriage *c.* 1930, next a post-war, flat-sided Hawksworth second-class carriage. The train justifies its express status by way of stopping at only a few stations east of Reading. Castles, Halls, 61xxs, and even the occasional Churchward or Collett mogul could be rostered for such duties.

Above: No. 4096 *Highclere Castle*, which has brought in the empty stock of an express for Bristol, and No. 6005 *King George II*, which has brought in the 7.30 a.m. from Shrewsbury, simmer away on platforms eight and nine respectively, 24 March 1951. A fine row of London taxis, many of them, the more upright ones, of pre-war origin, await passengers. The London taxi has always been a unique institution and although many have been sold elsewhere, all over the world indeed, they remain as potent a symbol of the capital as the red double-decker bus. This was a period when they were much in demand second hand, having been maintained to the high standards demanded by the Metropolitan Police. One such owner was my English teacher in 1951–52, an Australian, Mr Merry. For company in the school car park, it had the headmaster's large American Buick, and woodwork teacher Chips Brierley's Humber estate car with wooden framing, all out of the ordinary run of Austins, Morris's, Fords, Hillmans, and the like. Incidentally, the vast majority of London taxis were Austins. (*Brian Morrison*)

Below: The scene that would greet intending passengers as they came down into the station from Praed Street. Directly ahead would be express engines just arrived from the Midlands or the West Country, while over to the left would be pannier tanks and the empty stock of departing expresses. Here, No. 5094 *Tretower Castle* has just arrived at platform eight with an express from Cheltenham and Gloucester on 20 May 1957, alongside No. 5943 *Elmdon Hall* at platform seven.

If allowing the Western Region to apply chocolate and cream livery to a surprising number of its allocated main line carriages, and green livery, complete with lining out, even to tank engines, was not a sufficient turning back of the clock, in 1957, the historic, record-breaking 4-4-0 *City of Truro* was released from York Railway Museum, restored to steam, and let lose all over former Great Western metals, and some others too. Based at Didcot, it is seen here at the head of an RCTS special (note the admirably discrete headboard), surrounded by devoted admirers at Paddington. (*Brian Morrison*)

When not employed on special duties, it was encouraged to earn its keep working a commuter train into Paddington on weekday mornings, returning during the evening rush hour. It is seen here approaching Old Oak Common in 1958 with a very mundane train of seven non-corridor carriages, a number of them BR standards, and one corridor carriage, the sixth, presumably first class with access to a lavatory. (*Author's collection*)

Left: The *City of Truro* would retire to Old Oak Common for servicing and is seen here on a very wet day, 18 August 1958, where it would no doubt have felt quite a home among its copper-capped brethren, although not many would have been about when it was withdrawn from normal service in 1931. Once production of Castles and Halls had got into full swing, and the Stars and Saints were gradually being downgraded, there was little work for the big wheeled 4-4-0s. The *City of Truro* was spared breaking up for it might, or might not, have been the first locomotive, indeed the first manmade object, to achieve 100 mph, in May 1904.

Below: To complete this saga of one of the Great Western Railway's most famous pieces of rolling stock is this picture of it in its final preserved condition, as No. 3717, the number it carried between 1912 and 1931, in steam at the National Railway Museum, York, shortly before it ceased active service in 2012. It can presently be seen at STEAM, the Museum of the Great Western Railway at its birthplace, Swindon.

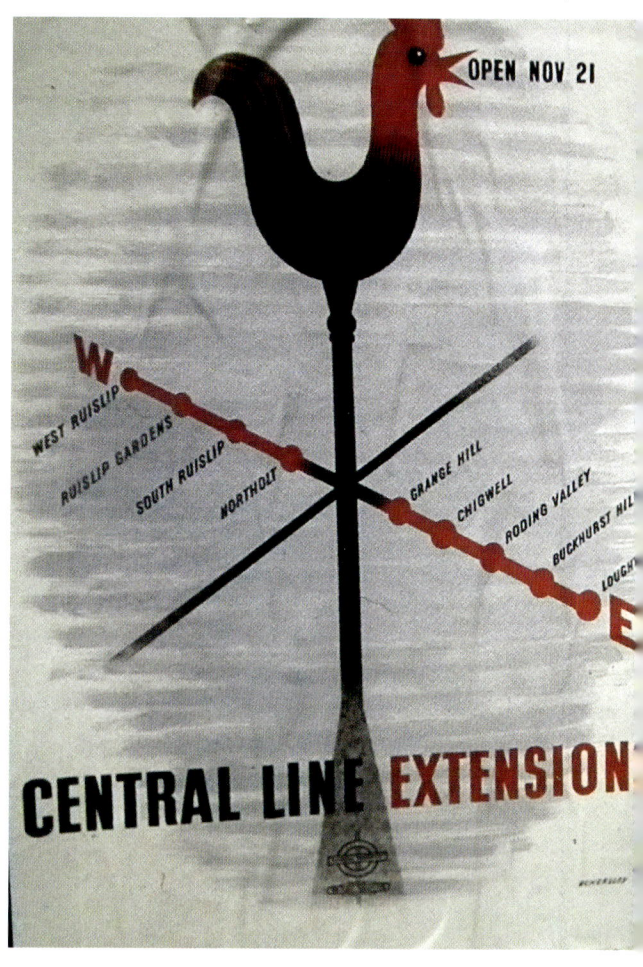

Above left: Metroland poster. We are now heading off into the wilds of Acton, not quite bandit country—more the fringes of Metroland, so take courage. If you have seen John Betjeman's wonderful film of *Metro-land*, you will recall that he goes to a ladies' club lunch in Pinner. The impression one gets of these ladies is that they could have taken on a whole Panzer division with one hand tied behind their backs. (*Author's collection*)

Above right: Tube poster. The section from South Ruislip was built jointly by the GWR and the Great Central Railway in 1906, the latter coming in from Marylebone at Northolt Junction, and suburban services were provided by the GCR and its successors, as well as the GWR. In the 1930s, the Central line was planned to be extended to Denham, thus leaving no need for steam-hauled services in and out of Paddington. In the event, the Second World War held up construction but it resumed in 1945 and a year later, tube trains reached as far as Greenford, then West Ruislip in 1947. This became the terminus, the creation of the Green Belt meaning Denham remained basically rural. The Central line did not serve Paddington; the nearest Central line stations being Lancaster Gate and Queensway, each roughly a mile distant. (*Author's collection*)

Above: A joint Great Western and Great Central Railways chair in place at the preserved railway at Quainton Road, once a far-flung outpost of the GCR's partner, the Metropolitan Railway.

Below: Any suburban steam journeys I made on that line were to and from Marylebone. The area being rather upmarket, the LNER/Eastern Region did not subject its clients to the rigours of the articulated stock common at Liverpool Street and Kings Cross but used sets of reasonably spacious non-corridor carriages similar in general design to those found on the Thames Valley services at Paddington. This picture shows just how joint the line was. One of the 61xx 2-6-2Ts, introduced by the GWR in 1931 specifically for the London area suburban services, is seen at Sudbury Hill hauling six Eastern Region carriages, five Gresleys, and one ex-GCR one on a down stopper out of Marylebone in 1949. (*Author's collection*)

Above: After the war, the LNER Thompson-designed L1 2-6-4Ts provided the principal motive power on Great Central line suburban trains until replaced by DMUs. Handsome locomotives, they took over from the equally handsome and rather more successful Robinson-designed Great Central A5 4-6-2Ts. It is difficult to put the finger on just why the L1s were something of a failure, but they had short lives and none were preserved. This is No. 67781 near Beaconsfield. (*Brian Morrison*)

Below: Princes Risborough box, about to be taken out of service in March 1992, but now preserved. Princes Risborough was the junction where the Great Central expresses for Aylesbury and beyond diverged, and is today where the preserved Chinnor and Princes Risborough Railway connects.

Above: Since 2017, Chiltern Trains have run services from Oxford to Marylebone by way of a new link at Bicester to the old Great Western main line. A view from inside a London-bound commuter train at Princes Risborough in September 2017.

Below: Post-war, the Eastern Region sent some A3 pacifics over to the Great Central, thus recalling the first meeting of a Gresley pacific and a Great Western Castle, at the British Empire Exhibition in 1925. The fastest of all Gresley's pacifics, indeed the fastest steam locomotive in the world, no less, A4 No. 4468 *Mallard*, at Marylebone on a special headed for the High Wycombe line in the 1982.

Above: The title of this book does, of course, focus on Paddington but Marylebone has a significant part to play in our story, as we shall see. For twenty-five years, until 1973, it was administered by the Western Region. Much less grand a building than Paddington, it was nevertheless well designed—by the Great Central Railway Civil Engineer Henry William Braddock—and rather elegant as epitomised by the canopy protecting arriving passengers from the elements. Opened in 1899, it could only afford two platforms to begin with, as traffic was sparse. Indeed, it was threatened with closure in the 1960s, but today is busier than ever, not least on account of the enterprise of Chiltern Railways.

Below: The lines out of Paddington and Marylebone meet at Northolt Junction. In this 1982 scene, there are GWR-style lower quadrant semaphores aplenty. A Central line 1962 stock train has just begun its journey to Epping. The track in the foreground is the down line from Marylebone, the next two are the up and down Paddington tracks, while the up Marylebone line is out of sight on the far left.

Above: Swinging the camera around, we see a Marylebone-bound DMU, two of the carriages in dull rail blue, the other two in the rather more fetching, replacement blue and grey livery. On the left is a Liverpool Street-bound Central line tube train. Do not ask what I was doing between the two electrified lines.

Below: West Ruislip station *c*. 1980, still with its brown Western Region running board. A High Wycombe to Marylebone DMU is about to depart from beneath the rather brutalist late 1940s overbridge and buildings. The two central tracks were provided for the non-stop expresses to and from Paddington and Marylebone, which were prominent by their absence by this time. Out of the picture to the left is the Central line terminus. It was intended that the Underground trains would continue on to Denham and evidence of this still existed.

Above: North Acton Station, 10 June 1982. To the left, out of sight, are the Western Region main line tracks to Birmingham and beyond. North Acton station was built by the GWR in 1923. In 1947, it passed to the Central line of the Underground and in 1992, a third track and platform face was added, resulting in the demolition of the original station buildings. Beyond is the North London line from Willesden Junction to Richmond and then the Western Region main line to Reading and the West. The next stations are East Acton and then White City. The Tube train will pass through the heart of London and continue on former LNER tracks to Stratford East and Epping.

Below: A Collett 2251 class 0-6-0 quite a long way from home. Gloucester-based No. 2290 passes Denham West Junction signal box on 11 April 1953 as it crosses the Grand Union Canal with a freight bound for Neasden yard. No. 2290s tender looks a good deal more ancient than No. 2290 itself, which dates from the mid-1930s, the tender being of the Dean era. Kings have been recorded on up expresses belting past Denham in excess of 100 mph: no danger of No. 2290 being so tempted. (*Brian Morrison*)

Above: In almost ex-works condition, No. 5907 *Marble Hall* heads a Gloucester-bound freight past Denham on 11 April 1953. Although black-lined British Railways suited the Halls quite well, much was the delight of Western enthusiasts when Swindon began turning out all its mixed traffic 4-6-0s in lined green (including BR Standards) at the end of 1955. (*Brian Morrison*)

Below: A GWR 28xx 2-8-0 passing High Wycombe with a down freight train, 1947. These Churchward-designed locomotives, the first of which came out in 1903, set the standard for the heavy freight locomotive throughout the UK and remained in production into the 1940s. Note the LNER carriages in the background. (*Author's collection*)

Above: High Wycombe station looking towards London from the end of the up platform in December 1988, with no shortage of pure Great Westernry in the mile post, lower quadrant signals, and signal box.

Below: Looking in the other direction, we can see what all the excitement was about. British Rail had decided to operate several steam-hauled 'Santa Specials' out of Marylebone that Christmas. The two locomotives, involved and seen here at High Wycombe, were LNER A4 pacific No. 4498 *Sir Nigel Gresley*, and SR-rebuilt Merchant Navy pacific No. 35028 *Clan Line*.

Above: Brand new 165012, one of the Thames Turbo suburban units, dating from 1990–92, which has become as synonymous as the 61xx tank engines, once with Western Region London area services, enters High Wycombe on 12 March 1992.

Below: No. 6123, 2-6-2T, approaches High Wycombe from the south, with a stopping train from Maidenhead. The section of this line, from Bourne End to High Wycombe, was closed in 1970. (*Brian Morrison*)

Above: No. 4082 *Windsor Castle* has charge of the funeral train of King George VI as it approaches Slough and the branch for Windsor on 15 February 1952. The locomotive is not the real Windsor Castle which was at that time undergoing overhaul in Swindon Works. Instead, one of the post-war Castles, No. 7013 *Bristol Castle* assumed its identity. The carriages are a mixture of North Eastern, Great Northern, and London and North Eastern Railway origin. (*Brian Morrison*)

Below: A rather more joyful occasion at Windsor. The flags are out at the Western Region station to celebrate the Coronation of Queen Elizabeth in June 1953. A Thames Valley Bristol/ECW double-decker bus awaits passengers. (*Author's collection*)

Above: For a while, there was a wonderful exhibition, mounted by Madame Tussauds in the GWR station at Windsor, recreating the arrival of Queen Victoria in 1897, and this included a non-working replica of the Dean single No. 3041 *The Queen*, attached to a royal saloon of 1897, was rescued from service as a holiday home at Aberporth. Sadly, there was more money to be made by turning the whole area into retail outlets, although the locomotive, minus tender remains. The carriage is now to be found at STEAM, the museum of the GWR in Swindon.

Below: Heading back down the High Wycombe to Paddington main line (except it is not much of a main line anymore), this is Greenford East signal box; it is special because in 2017, it was the very last operational GWR signal box in the London area and controlled a cluster of lower quadrant semaphore signals. It stands beside what was the GWR main line from Paddington to the north, but this section is now a mere single track and the main line station here, a typical one with looped platforms, closed in 1963. However, there is certainly still a Greenford station, one that serves the Central line and also the former GWR branch service from the West of England main line at Ealing.

This is a westbound Central line 1992-stock train arriving at Greenford, 19 May 2003. Very different visually to their predecessors with vastly more window space, at both front and side, they were built at BREL, Derby, although two of the four prototypes were made in Birmingham by Metro-Cammell. Cheaper and lighter, being constructed from wide aluminium extrusions welded together, they were a welcome, colourful, return to innovation.

Next up comes a Class 165 Thames Turbo from Ealing. First class was abandoned in these units in 2015, an indication of rising passenger numbers and overcrowding.

Left: An innovation that failed was the Wrexham and Shropshire service out of Marylebone, which began in 2008. Various restrictions meant trains could only call at certain stations and then only picking up, the first stop was Banbury, and neither Birmingham New Street nor Birmingham Snow Hill, for example, featured. The carriages were refurbished Mark IIIs, the motive power 67s, which meant a welcome return of locomotive-hauled passenger trains to the route. There were five trains a day in each direction, taking approximately four hours and fifteen minutes. Hopes were pinned on the restoration of a direct London to Shrewsbury service but in the event, the service proved uneconomic and ended in January 2011.

Below: This was one of the carriages: a first downgraded to standard. It offered much the most comfortable journey I had experienced in years. An elderly lady who joined at Banbury with her knitting, remarked that 'this is a wonderful service', which she used regularly to visit a friend in Wrexham. It was all very John Betjeman. It has to be admitted that there were only five passengers in the train when we left Marylebone. There was also a guard, three members of staff in the buffet car, and, of course, a driver.

Above: Continuing our journey northwards brings us to Banbury with No. 66501 at the head of a Freightliner train standing on what remains of the once extensive sidings where the work of sorting traffic from the north of England and the Midlands, brought in on the Great Central line from Rugby, once carried on twenty-four hours a day, seven days a week. There may be fewer trains about but there are plenty of men in orange suits.

Below: Banbury on 8 August 1959. No. 6874 *Haughton Grange* is at the head of a 'Summer Saturday' train from the South Coast to Birmingham. Alongside is former LNER K3 2-6-0 No. 61852, which will leave on one of the infrequent stopping trains from Banbury to Rugby Central. It was freight that made this link so vital and beyond the two passenger trains is an up goods, with an LMS-built guard's van bringing up the rear, while freight wagons stretch far into the distance on the extensive sidings. The father on the far right would appear be taking the baby to have look at the Grange.

Above: Each summer weekend, the Shakespeare Express steam trains operate between Birmingham Snow Hill and Moor Street to Stratford-upon-Avon. No. 4965 *Rood Ashton Hall*, based at Tyseley, pauses at Moor Street before its final destination, Snow Hill. The reconstructed Moor Street is as close a recreation of the Great Western era it is possible to get on the modern railway system. It was the terminus of suburban trains from the south, the two main line through tracks passing it on their way into the tunnel leading to Snow Hill. Threatened with closure in the late 1970s, the world shifted on its axis back to common sense, as in 1984, funds were secured both for the reopening of Snow Hill and the transformation of Moor Street. For the revival of the latter, Chiltern Railways built new platforms beside the through tracks; a wonderful recreation of what the railway's chairman, Adrian Shooter, described as 'the best inner city railway station in the country' reaped numerous awards.

Below: In the last days of steam, Kings did run right through from Paddington to Shrewsbury, on the Cambrian Coast Express. No. 6013 *King Henry VIII* entered Shrewsbury past the very famous and listed LNWR-designed Severn Bridge signal box, now the largest manually operated signal box in the world, in September 1961. Just visible on the far left of the picture is the Manor class 4-6-0, which will take the train to west Wales.

Right: The afternoon departure to Marylebone gets right away from Wrexham in September 2009.

Below: Churchward mogul No. 6311 waits for the road at Wolvercote Junction where the lines from Banbury and Worcester converge north of Oxford with a lengthy goods train in 1962. (*Hedley Sparks*)

Above: The GWR, once much addicted to the 4-4-0, got close to wiping out this wheel arrangement by the end of the 1930s, the only survivors being a handful of Dukes and Bulldogs, both being classified as mixed traffic locomotives, plus, of course the rather extraordinary 9xxxs, allegedly a new build, but were actually Duke boilers mounted on Bulldog frames. The very last Bulldog, No. 3454 *Skylark*, is seen at Oxford station on a Stephenson Locomotive Society special composed of five carriages of much more modern vintage, shortly before its withdrawal in November 1951. (*Author's collection*)

Below: Another veteran very near the end of its days is Star No. 4061 *Glastonbury Abbey*, seen here at Oxford on 8 August 1956. Based at Stafford Road shed, it has brought in a train from Wolverhampton and is about to hand over to No. 5012 *Berry Pomeroy Castle*, which will take it on to Paddington. The *Glastonbury Abbey* was withdrawn in March 1957, the penultimate Star, the very last being No. 4056 *Princess Margaret*, which lasted until November of that year.

Above: June 1956 saw the author posted to RAF Abingdon, after completion of training as a less than totally competent typist at RAF Hereford. This was pretty decent of the Air Ministry, both venues being in former Great Western territory. Hence, with a generous amount of spare time, there being far more National Servicemen than the RAF knew what to do with, there was plenty of time to observe steam at work. I got to travel fairly regularly on Hereford line expresses and here Paddington-bound Castle No. 5083 *Bath Abbey* (really a rebuilt Star) has got well into its stride after the Oxford stop, hurtling past Churchward 2-8-0 2835 waiting patiently in the loop at Radley on 19 September 1956.

Below: Churchward's nine 47xx 2-8-0s were quite unique, being the only UK freight engines of this wheel arrangement that were also capable of regularly hauling long distance passenger trains, something they did throughout their long careers, but especially at the very end notwithstanding a considerable number of diesel locomotives being at work on the Western Region. Here on 22 July 1961, No. 4705 is approaching Reading from the west with a train composed entirely of GWR carriages, with the odd LMS interloper. A little earlier, No. 4706 had sped through Reading, non-stop, in charge of the 1.25 p.m. Paddington to Kingswear. You might like to count the lower quadrant semaphore signals.

Above: The very first main line Western Region diesel-hydraulics were the five members of the North British type 4 A1A-A1A Warship class diesel-hydraulics. Huge lumbering beasts, they were outdated virtually before they were delivered in 1958 from the doomed North British Locomotive Company. All five were withdrawn by 1967, at a time when several hundred steam locomotives were still at work on BR. D603 Conquest is leaving Reading on 1 August 1989 with the 11.05 a.m. Paddington to Penzance.

Below: By summer 1959, all the West of England main line expresses had officially gone over to diesel haulage. However, diesel unreliability meant that Kings and Castles in particular had to be on standby and here on 1 August 1959, No. 6029 *King Edward VIII* has charge of the Royal Duchy. This locomotive only acquired its name when Edward VIII ascended to the throne in 1935 but kept it, even though the King by 1937 had been demoted, or rather demoted himself, to Duke of Windsor.

Above: Twyford, 5 July 1951. No. 4948 *Northwick Hall* has charge of a Henley-on-Thames to Paddington special and is rapidly being overtaken by No. 5020 *Tremartion Castle* at the head of the up the Red Dragon from South Wales. This is before the first BR standard carriages were to be seen in any numbers on the Western Region; indeed, the first and last non-corridor carriages of the train from Henley are still in rather faded GWR chocolate and cream as are some of the carriages of the Red Dragon. (*Brian Morrison*)

Below: Southall was the last active steam depot on the Western Region in the London area. A number of locomotives withdrawn from Old Oak Common were moved there before their last journey to the scrapyard. However, No. 5042 *Winchester Castle*, minus its nameplates, was officially a Gloucester engine when withdrawn a day or two before I took this picture on 13 June 1965. It is coupled to a Collett 2-8-0.

Above: There remained a fair bit of work, mostly mundane goods, in this final steam summer of 1965. From left to right, there is a glimpse of a DMU, then a Modified Hall, a 61xx, a Stanier 8F 2-8-0, a Collett 2884 2-8-0, and two 08 diesel shunters.

Below: Close-up of a BR Standard 9F 2-10-0, one of a class very much in the 47xx tradition, chiefly designed for hauling heavy freight but well able to reach 80 mph and more on passenger workings, and the inevitable 61xx.

Above: In earlier days, this little Collett 1932 vintage 14xx 0-4-2T had been shedded at Southall and worked the Greenford branch. Yet another survivor preserved at Didcot, it holds a very special place in the story of GWR preservation.

Below: In 1962, four sixteen-year-old Southall schoolboys decided that a 14xx really had to be preserved; they placed an appeal to this end in *The Railway Magazine*, money poured in, and, scarcely before they knew it and not quite sure what they had let themselves in for, they found themselves owner of 1466, which would become the very first locomotive in the unique collection of the Great Western Society at Didcot. It is seen here working with one of the post-war Hawksworth design auto coaches.

Above: Jon Barlow, one of the original four sixteen-year olds, is still regularly to be seen at Didcot. Here he is in charge of No. 3440 *City of Truro*.

Below: A first generation DMU working the Greenford branch near South Greenford in 1985.

Right: No. 5081 *Lockheed Hudson* speeds through Southall with a Paddington to Worcester and Hereford express on 5 May 1956. The train is passing under the footbridge upon which the four founder members of the Great Western Society regularly met to watch the trains go by. Such is its significance in the history of GWR preservation that when it was recently replaced, a section of it was given by Railtrack to the Great Western Society to live on in perpetuity at Didcot Rail Centre. No. 5081 was one of twelve Castle class 4-6-0s, which were given the names of RAF aircraft during the Second World War. (*Brian Morrison*)

Below: One of the Collett moguls, No. 7328 of 1932, takes hold of what claims to be an express but which I am almost certain is empty stock passing Subway Junction on 18 April 1960. The third carriage is a 70-foot-long Edwardian-era Dreadnought restaurant car, refurbished by Hamptons and generally brought up to date in the 1930s.

89

Above: No. 92220 9F 2-10-0 was named *Evening Star* in a ceremony at Swindon Works in March 1960 to mark the launch of the very last steam locomotive for British Rail. Adorned in lined green with a copper cap chimney, it worked from Cardiff Canton depot. I happened to visit Paddington on 27 June that year and was astonished to capture this photo of *Evening Star*, complete with headboard, backing out, having just brought in the Red Dragon from Swansea. The 9Fs were heavy freight locomotives so I assumed it must have been a last-minute substitute for a Britannia 4-6-2—not a bit of it. For five days, until 1 July, the 2-10-0 performed this duty, on the first occasion, so legend has it, getting so far ahead of schedule that it had to slow for the refreshment car to be cleared. The authorities then ordered normality to be restored and the *Evening Star* banished back to freight duties. The 9Fs, whenever they got the chance, proved they could really speed. I recall a journey behind *Evening Star* in preservation days when we were assured it had exceeded 80 mph, although, as the crew remarked, they could not be sure 'all the wheels were touching the rails'. It is a long time since No. 92220 has been allowed on the main line. It was a tragedy that such magnificent locomotives arrived so late on the steam scene and that, unlike in France and Germany, provision was not made for them to work out their normal lifespan.

Below: The first of the Swindon-built Warships diesel-hydraulics, D800 *Sir Brian Robertson* passing Subway Junction on 21 March 1959 with an express from Plymouth. Much better looking than the original North British A1A-A1As, and a rather better machine, they were given the classification type 42. A further thirty-three type 43s were actually built by North British. These type 43s had engines and transmissions built by North British, while the Swindon-built ones had German MAN engines. The 42s and 43s looked almost identical, but the latter were less reliable. For various reasons, hydraulic transmission had fallen out of favour by the end of the 1960s, and the 43s passed to the scrapheap before the 42s, two of which have been preserved.

Above: In 1962, virtually in one swoop, the entire King class was withdrawn, straight from top link duties. Their successors were the Western Class 52 diesel-hydraulics. Here we see the first, D1000 Western Enterprise, having arrived at Paddington with the Midland Pullman, which was normally worked by one of the Blue Pullman units. In this case, a varied collection of locomotive-hauled of Pullmans and non-Pullmans has been substituted. More on the Westerns later. (*Author's collection*)

Below: The last regular steam-hauled passenger train out of Paddington was scheduled for Friday, 11 June 1965. This is a Subway Junction picture of No. 7029 *Clun Castle* backing down to the terminus, passing a Western Class 52 heading in the opposite direction for South Wales.

Above: A short while later, 7029 came pounding back, this time in charge of the 4.15 p.m. to Banbury, the very last ordinary scheduled steam service out of Paddington, thus ensuring *Clun Castle*'s place in railway history. The next year, Patrick Whitehouse made sure it would join the already officially preserved pioneer Castle, No. 4073 *Caerphilly Castle*, by buying it for £2,400 and over the years, it has made many journeys from its base at Tyseley in Birmingham. There would be several more preserved Castles, eventually.

Below: The *Clun Castle* about to pass under Great Western Road. The first carriage is a BR Mark I brake composite; the rest of the train a mixture of Mark 1s and LMS-designed corridors, but nothing of GWR origin.

Above: One of the Great Western Society's first purchases, after the little 0-4-2T 1466, was 61xx 2-6-2T No. 6106. It is seen here, on Southall shed in the summer of 1965, already polished and shining ready for its new life.

Below: No. 7808 *Cookham Manor* was also bought straight of service, by a Great Western Society member, the only one of the original 1938 Manors to survive. It is seen passing through Sonning Cutting on 17 September 1966, returning to Birmingham after a visit to a GWS open day at Taplow. (*Charles Whetmath*)

Above: The GWR diesel railcars of the 1930s and early 1940s were the first really successful examples of a form of motive power that would become commonplace from the mid-1950s onwards. Seen at Didcot are two preserved examples. No. 4, part of the National Collection administered by the Science Museum, is one of the original Park Royal-bodied vehicles of 1934. Wonderfully streamlined, it attracted the nickname *Flying Banana*. No. 22 dates from 1940 and, while equally stylish, it goes in for straight edges. It lives at Didcot and has been in almost continuous service there, apart from the odd visit elsewhere, for over forty years.

Below: Paddington in 1969. No. 47078 *Daniel Gooch*, a Brush type 4 diesel-electric in its original two-tone livery, alongside a conversation being conducted between the guard of a Paignton-bound express and the train driver in charge of Class 52 No. 1035 *Western Yeoman*.

Above: The Hymeks looked like no other main line diesel, especially when first introduced. Just because dark green with orange and black lining perfectly suited ex-GWR locomotives, it did not mean this livery would be ideal for all other steam engines, and certainly not diesels—far from it. The Hymeks were the exception to the rule, at least as the dark green is concerned, and as this view of the preserved D7018 at Didcot shows how, allied with a nice band of pale green below decks, plenty of white around the cab, and red buffers to go with the dark green, was distinctly pleasing.

Below: The later colour scheme of rail blue with all yellow fronts did the Hymek design no favours as this view of three lined up at Old Oak Common *c.* 1971 demonstrates.

Above: A Warship gets under way passing the Paddington parcel platform as it accelerates westwards with its train of ten Mk 1 carriages. It is clearly a warm summer day, *c.* 1972.

Below: Milk from the west of England was once a significant traffic on the GWR/WR. Tankers from various originating stations would be brought each evening to Kensington Olympia, and then worked over the West London line to their destination at the Wood Lane depot in Acton. The train of empties here is hauled by Warship 807 *Caradoc* on 4 October 1971 and is coming off the West London line at North Pole Junction heading back to the West Country for a refill.

Above: On a bright, sunny afternoon in 1973, No. 1025 *Western Guardsman* gets the right away with a Paddington to Cardiff express. Completed in November 1963, *Western Guardsman* was withdrawn in January 1979. Any time one espied a large cloud of acrid smoke hovering over the Paddington area between 1962 and 1979, it was likely that a Western was beneath it, probably smirking as it got a grip of its westbound express; Westerns liked to make their presence felt.

Below: With a roof line that echoes the shape of the station arch, a Western is grumbling away to itself, eager to be off to South Wales on a summer afternoon in 1971.

Above: Old Oak Common, July 1974. A Western, in blue livery and a 47, still in its by now rather careworn original two-tone green livery, wait to enter the depot while another Western speeds past with an up express composed of a mixture of BR Mark 1 and Mark 11A carriages.

Below: With the famous (or perhaps infamous) final fifteen guinea steam run in the north-west of England, departing and returning to Liverpool Lime Street in August 1968, steam was officially banned from the BR network. Steam was yesterday; today and tomorrow are electric and diesel. Yet, rather like trying to tie down a safety valve on a steam locomotive, enforcing the ban proved impossible, such was the pressure and, fittingly—no bias there—it was the GWR's flagship No. 6000 *King George V* that in October 1971 made a triumphant return to the main line. It is seen here at Old Oak Common, having come down the main line from Birmingham and was on its way to be on display to the public at Kensington Olympia.

Above: *King George V*, since its retirement in 1962, had been based at Hereford, being partly funded by Bulmers Cider, near the old locomotive depot. Bulmers had also preserved five Pullman cars, which formed part of the *King George V* brought to London.

Below: Carriages of pre-nationalisation disappeared much the same time as steam ended—we have seen there was not a single carriage of GWR design in the last steam-hauled train out of Paddington. Yet for some reason, despite being wooden-bodied, Gresley designed LNER-built restaurant/buffet cars found favour and proved to be particularly long lived; here is one, in rail blue and grey livery with a 'W' prefix at Paddington in 1970.

Similarly, passenger brakes and parcel vans tended to outlive their passenger-carrying contemporaries and in this 1970 selection at Old Oak Common carriage depot, there are vehicles of GWR, LMS, and SR origin. On the far right is one of the less than totally successful, rough-riding, Blue Pullman units, introduced in 1960. Moved to the Western Region in 1967, they were all withdrawn in 1973.

A newly transferred Class 50 and Western Class 52 No. 1058 *Western Nobleman* meet in 1974 by Old Oak Common engine shed signal box, which had the longest nameplate of any former GWR box. The Class 50s displaced the Westerns, No. 1058 being the last to be scrapped after withdrawal in July 1979. Inevitably, the Class 50s acquired the nickname 50/50s, which was a bit unfair as they were reasonably reliable and acquired an enthusiast following. They were not, however, very long lived—apart from preserved examples.

Above: The Class 31s, originally built at the very beginning of the diesel era and known as the Brush Type 2s, replaced the Hymeks and other lower-powered North British diesel-hydraulic locomotives. Originally associated with the Eastern Region, they, like the HSTs, were among the best buys BR ever acquired—and BR bought some real turkeys; some remained on front line duties for over fifty years. One is seen here shunting the Old Oak Common breakdown train, the crane itself being steam-powered, the engineering department coach being a converted Southern Railway 'Ironclad' dating from the 1920s.

Below: OOC turntable. The diesel era saw Old Oak Common depot reduced in size and much altered with the former roundhouse buildings removed leaving the turntable exposed to the elements. From left to right: a Hymek, a Class 50, and a Class 47 in 1973.

Above: Hymek 7055 pulls out of Paddington in 1971 with a South Wales express, a service that the Hymeks inherited (but not for long) from the King, Castle, and Britannia class steam locomotives. Withdrawals began in 1971, marking the beginning of the end for the Hymeks.

Below: As the Western withdrawal gathered pace, there were numerous commemorative tours. The last, sad, but also celebratory day of the Westerns in ordinary service arrived on 26 February 1977. Any uninformed innocent who assumed that with the end of steam, locospotting and the time-honoured practice of collecting at the platform ends at Paddington and elsewhere simply to observe trains coming and going would fade away had not taken into account the Western phenomenon. Letting rip with an explosion of power and enough smoke, exhaust, and burned fuel oil to add several hundred more members to Friends of the Earth, the two locomotives accelerated with the very last Western-hauled train out of Paddington, the *Western Tribute*, bound for Swansea, Plymouth, and back to Paddington. (*Brian Morrison*)

Above: The *Western Tribute* seen passing Old Oak Common and assembled photographers and observers a few minutes later. Both locomotives went straight into preservation, *Western Ranger* finding a home on the Severn Valley Railway.

Below: Meanwhile, the Great Western Society, having established itself at Didcot, was going from strength to strength. Here is Modified Hall No. 6998 *Burton Agnes Hall*, bought in 1966 straight from service at Oxford Shed, having hauled the Western Region's last steam train.

Above: The GWS, established at the beginning of the preservation scene, bought a number of GWR-design carriages, also straight from service. With an enthusiastic volunteer work force, it had the numbers and skills to bring them up to main line standard and in October 1972, the first two ventured out, from Paddington to Didcot, where *Burton Agnes Hall* took over, for the run to Stratford-upon-Avon. By 1976, the number of carriages had grown to eight and a second Hall, No. 5900 *Hinderton Hall*, had been rescued and restored to steam from Woodhams scrap yard at Barry Island. Here, the two Halls are heading past the cooling towers of Didcot power station on 15 May 1976. As was the usual practice, the train had started from Paddington with diesel power, steam taking over at Didcot. (*Charles Whetmath*)

Below: Eventually, no fewer than ten chocolate-and-cream-liveried carriages were passed for main line running and here, on 1 October 1978, No. 7808 *Cookham Manor* and No. 5900 *Hinderton Hall*, having reversed out of the railway centre, are entering Didcot station prior to a run to Tyseley Steam Centre. Right at the end of the train are two of the magnificent, wide-bodied Super Saloons, built for the Plymouth boat trains—the epitome of 1930s luxury.

A view from the footplate of Cookham Manor at Banbury station 1 October 1978, the two locomotives taking on water there.

The number of preserved Castle-class 4-6-0s was growing. No. 5051 *Earl Bathurst*, which had also used the name *Drysllwyn Castle*, was rescued from Barry in 1970 and restored to working order in January 1980. No. 5051 was passed for main line running just in time to take charge of the final run on the Vintage Train of preserved and restored GWR-designed carriages on the main line. It is seen here, turned out temporarily in unlined wartime livery, on a trail run as far as Oxford. (*Charles Whetmath*)

Above: The very last run of the Vintage Train on the main line was on 26 January 1980. In this view, it stands at platform six, Paddington, waiting for the off. The amount of work needed to keep ten vintage carriages up to the rigorous standards for main line work put a tremendous strain on Didcot's volunteers. To do it for as long as they did was a remarkable achievement, but it could not last. Nearest the camera are the two Super Saloons. The bearded figure leaning out is Graham Perry, one of the original founder members, holder of membership No. 1 and for many years was chairman of the GWS.

Below: The weather was grey and overcast when we left Paddington but the skies were clearing—naturally enough, after all GWR also stood for God's Wonderful Railway—as No. 5051 took over from the Class 31 diesel at Didcot. The train is seen here approaching Stratford-upon-Avon in bright winter sunshine. (*Charles Whetmath*)

Above: Fewer than three months later, chocolate and cream carriages and Swindon-built steam locomotives were back at Paddington. On 11 March 1979, the station celebrated its 125th birthday. At first glance, this might seem to be a steam-age picture with two GWR-design carriages and steam rising from a locomotive at the buffer stops. These were two preserved carriages from Didcot headed by No. 5900 *Hinderton Hall*.

Below: *Hinderton Hall*, bearing an appropriate train reporting number, with a Class 50 diesel-electric locomotive playing a minor role on each occasion.

Above: The Western Region authorities entered fully into the spirit of the occasion and some of the ticket collectors donned appropriate vintage apparel.

Below: If this was not sufficient, No. 6000 *King George V* graciously agreed to take charge of a special train from Paddington to Didcot. It is seen here backing down watched by vast crowds and more than one HST. (*John Titlow*)

Above: Plenty of room on a King's footplate as he prepares for the right away. The tables in the train were provided with vases full of daffodils, a reminder that spring was on the way. Unfortunately, *King George V* rather blotted its copy book, being declared at Didcot unfit to return to the capital and a Class 47 had to be substituted. The next morning's edition of the *Daily Mail*, on the ball as ever, sagely hoped that the King would 'not have to be scrapped'.

Below: Here is *Iron Duke* alongside No. 6000 *King George V* at Old Oak Common, both the subjects of admiring crowds.

Above: *Iron Duke* again, this time alongside Stanier ex-LMS pacific No. 46229 *Duchess of Hamilton*. Stanier was, of course, a Swindon man and, with the wind in the right direction, his pacifics could be heard from Old Oak Common, hooting as they steamed through Willesden Junction, a mile away.

Below: To get to Old Oak Common, the powers that be kindly provided a train that started from the parcels platform at Paddington station, beyond platform one. This was something to be savoured for never before had I been able to travel, by train, from Paddington to Old Oak Common, there never being, of course, a station of that name. The locomotive provided was none other than No. 92220 *Evening Star*, the very last steam locomotive ever to be completed for British Rail. Here it is being passed by a HST in original livery.

Above: Only a fisherman could be so absorbed in studying the muddy waters of the Grand Union Canal, ignoring the rest of the world that had clambered on top of the canal wall to watch *Evening Star* steam over the bridge carrying the carriage road over the main line tracks.

Below: Three celebrity Class 47s in GWR green livery around the surviving turntable: No. 47484 *Isambard Kingdom Brunel*, No. 47078 *Sir Daniel Gooch*, and No. 47079 *George Jackson Churchward*.

Above: No. 5051 *Earl Bathurst* was at the other end of the shuttle between Old Oak Common and Paddington and is seen here leaving the depot and passing under the footbridge from the canal bank. This was an incomparable vantage point for studying the comings and goings to and from the locomotive and carriage depot. Did I ever sneak down it and into the depot? What do you think?

Below: Between 1994 and 2007, something even the far-sighted Brunel probably never imagined occupied the site of what had been the West London Works and carriage sidings east of where Scrubs Lane crosses the main line by Old Oak Common depot—Eurostar trains operating out of Waterloo to Paris and Brussels. The depot was in two sections (either side of Scrubs Lane), and in the eastern section are Eurostars with multi-hued HSTs on the Great Western main line beyond. With the transfer of the Eurostar London terminus from Waterloo to St Pancras, the depot was replaced by one at Temple Mills, near Stratford International. The Western depot is now the Hitachi depot for the new Great Western Class 800 bi-mode HST replacements.

Above: Two narrow boats head along the ever busy Regent's Canal passing two Eurostars in their North Pole depot.

Below: A Class 66 heads a freight past North Pole Junction and is about to pass over the bridge carrying the tracks on this enormously busy line over the Great Western main line and is heading towards Willesden Junction.

Above: A scene from the towpath of the Grand Union Canal alongside Old Oak Common depot as Class 66 heads north.

Below: Despite the disappearance of Paddington goods depot and all the little freight yards in the London area, the Great Western main line into London still carries an immense amount of bulk freight. A Class 70 is approaching West Drayton in October 2017 with a wonderfully assorted collection of containers.

Over the years, Old Oak Common locomotive depot gradually went into a state of not entirely dignified decline. You can see what I mean in this April 1996 picture of assorted derelict Class 47s and various other locomotives, some in states of distress and others still active.

A much happier prospect alongside is that of the HST depot at Old Oak Common in 2015 where one of the ever reliable and seemingly indestructible HSTs eases its way towards the main line past the Hitachi depot, which has replaced where Eurostars used to receive tender, loving care.

The Old Oak Common badge, worn by HSTs for a time c. 2014.

Eventually, Old Oak Common locomotive depot was razed to the grand. For a time, the site was used by CrossRail, an intimation of the enormous changes that are planned for the entire area when HS2, the high speed line from London to the Midlands and the North of England, comes into being.

Work on CrossRail goes ahead near Ladbroke Grove, September 2017.

Above: An Adelante Class 180, working a Cotswold line service, and a Paddington-bound HST pass at Old Oak Common in 2015. Built in 2000–01, the Class 180s were not totally successful and in 2009 were transferred away from the Western. However, five units were later returned specifically for Cotswold line services to Worcester and Hereford.

Below: One of the few exceptions to the HST rule is the overnight sleeping car train to and from Penzance. Here, deep into Cornwall and passing the remains of the mining industry at Carn Brea, is No. 57605 in charge of the 11.45 p.m. from Paddington on an August morning in 2010.

Above: A down HST, note the non matching carriage and power unit liveries—passes an up Heathrow express EMU at Ladbroke Grove, two miles out of Paddington in 1997. On 5 October 1999, thirty-one people died when a Bedwyn-bound Thames Turbo DMU crossed a signal at danger and was struck by an incoming HST. Between 1923 and 1948, the GWR had a superior safety record compared to the other Big Four, but this time, a combination of human error and a badly sighted signal proved fatal. By this date, the lines out of Paddington were, as far as Ladbroke Grove, bi-directional, with no more departure and arrival differentiation of platforms at Paddington; it was here they reverted to two up and two down lines.

Below: Eventually, only just in time to catch the twentieth century, despite the Wright Brothers having demonstrated that powered flight was possible quite a bit earlier, a direct, electrified, fast-surface railway link between Heathrow and central London was established, overhead wires appeared beneath Brunel's towering roof, and from 23 June 1998, a service of four trains an hour was inaugurated. Some 435 staff are employed by Heathrow Express, seventy-two being drivers. Later, in 2005, a cheaper stopping at every station, half hourly service began, the first stage of electrified commuter services in and out Paddington. Passengers bustle to and from Heathrow Expresses in November 2017.

Above: The site of Ranelagh depot, seen from Royal Oak station, in the autumn of 2017. Two Hammersmith line Underground trains are in the station with a HST and a Thames Turbo further away.

Below: In 2015, First Great Western became simply Great Western Railway and introduced a new, basically dark green livery, as can be seen on this Class 165 at Slough station in October 2017. Designed by Pentagram, it did not exactly meet with universal approval. Pentagram referred to original GWR traditions, but its carriages were never dark green and the initials 'GWR' were never portrayed in the manner chosen by Pentagram. However, in certain lighting conditions, it can all look appealing especially on the new Class 800 HST replacement express units, which Pentagram probably had in mind.

Above: Passengers alighting from a HST at Paddington in 2015.

Below: Passengers on platform one, Paddington, October 2017 (you might like to compare this with another platform picture, such as the one on page 20).

Above: One feature of the approach to Paddington was the series of impressive road bridges from the beginning of the twentieth century that span the tracks. By the start of the twenty-first century, Bishop's Road Bridge, which carried traffic over the country end of the platforms, had become a bottleneck and was replaced in 2004–6 by a six-lane highway, carried on giant steel beams: a feat of engineering ingenuity. In the process, Brunel's earliest surviving iron bridge, over the Regent's Canal, was discovered. It was removed and put into store to bring it back to the Paddington area and make a feature of it. Beyond are the tower blocks replacing Paddington goods station.

Below: On the east side of the station, there are some relatively unremarkable, but nevertheless distinguished, buildings that would disappear if a hideous tower block, mooted by developers and designed by Renzo Piano, he of the Shard, gets erected. Originally meant to be seventy-two storeys high, this was quickly scaled down, but in August 2017, planning permission was granted. However, the campaign group SAVE and other bodies have mounted a well-argued legal protest and one hopes they will succeed.

Above: SAVE had success in 2008 when proposals to demolish and replace the fourth span, right, of Paddington station were refused. This dates from 1913–15, a fine and very carefully crafted structure, 400 feet long, which complimented the original three spans. It was designed by William Armstrong, the GWR's chief engineer.

Below: Underground, GWR suburban, HST and Heathrow Express units, Paddington, 2016.

Looking down on the platform ends of Paddington station from the new Bishop's Road Bridge in October 2017. Dead centre is a Class 800 on its first day in service, flanked by HSTs. Prominent is the footbridge leading from the main line station to the suburban one in front of the four great spans including, far left, that was threatened by demolition in 2008.

Passing Royal Oak is electric unit No. 387144. Since spring 2017, these Bombardier, Derby-built units have been working between Paddington and Maidenhead, but they will eventually replace the Thames Turbo DMUs when the much-delayed Paddington suburban electrification scheme is up and running. The bridge looks as if it could do with some cosmetic care.

Above: A Class 800 bi-mode ready to depart from Paddington in October 2017 while the old order, represented by two HSTs, is on the opposite side of the station.

Below: Approaching Paddington in October 2017 at the rear of an HST from Bristol is the First World War memorial power car No. 43172 *Harry Patch*. Harry Patch, a native of Bath, was the last British survivor of the trench warfare of the First World War. Born in 1898, he was wounded at Passchendale in 1917 by a shell burst that killed three of his mates, and who he missed throughout his long life. He died at the age of 111 on 25 July 2009.

Above: The introduction of the 800s in October 2017 was accompanied by an imaginative advertising campaign, featuring Enid Blyton's *Famous Five*. This is the city theme poster.

Below: In September 2017, there was a grand open day at Old Oak Common depot. Featured in this picture by Frank Dumbleton, one of the original members of the Great Western Society, are, from left to right, the steam rail motor, based at Didcot, No. 6023 *King Edward II*, No. 7903 *Foremarke Hall*, Warship D821 *Greyhound*, Western No. 1015 *Western Champion*, No. 50035 *Ark Royal*, the original HST power car No. 253001, a Class 180 Adelante, and a Class 800 GWR express bi-mode unit. (*Frank Dumbleton*)

The seaside-themed poster, *The Famous Five*, and a Class 800 on the South Devon coast.

The 11.45 a.m. to Swansea about to depart, with two HSTs beyond, 17 October 2017.

Looking down on two Class 800 units, platform eight, Paddington, getting ready to depart for Newport, Cardiff, and Swansea on 17 October 2017.